LOST IN THE FOG

LOST IN THE FOG

MEMOIR OF A BASTARD

A BELGIAN REMEMBERS THE WAR, THE NAZIS, HER FRACTURED LIFE

Rachel Van Meers
as told to Daniel Chase

Academy Chicago Publishers

Published in 2008 by
Academy Chicago Publishers
363 West Erie Street
Chicago, Illinois 60610

Printed and bound in the U.S.A.

Library of Congress Cataloging-in-Publication Data

Van Meers, Rachel, 1930–
  Lost in the fog : memoir of a bastard / Rachel Van Meers as told to
Daniel Chase.
    p. cm.
  ISBN 978-0-89733-571-3 (pbk.)
  1. Van Meers, Rachel, 1930– 2. Flemish Americans—Biography. 3.
Belgian Americans—Biography. 4. Immigrants—United States—Biog-
raphy. 5. Illegitimate children—Belgium—Ghent—Biography. 6.
Working class—Belgium—Ghent—Biography. 7. Ghent (Belgium)—
Biography. 8. Ghent (Belgium)—Social conditions—20th century. 9.
World War, 1939-1945—Personal narratives, Belgian. 10. World War,
1939–1945—Belgium—Ghent. I. Chase, Daniel (Daniel Thomas) II.
Title.

E184.F57V36 2008
949.3'14203—dc22
                              2007046513

*"Why is it some people make such good books,
and I can't remember shit?"*
—Rachel Van Meers

ACKNOWLEDGMENTS

WE WOULD LIKE TO OFFER SPECIAL THANKS TO TAMMY JEBB, who helped with editing and consultation during various stages of this book's development, Robert Farrugia for his assistance with the photographs, and finally the support of all of our friends and family, without which this book would not have been possible.

CONTENTS

PREFACE

I was six years old when I first met Rachel Van Meers. My family moved into her house in Oregon and rented it for eleven years. It was a warm little house, tucked away in a small pocket of Madrones, full of secret places. I don't recall much about Rachel back then except that she seemed to be an extraordinarily happy person. Years later when I became truly acquainted with her and her story, I came to realize that she is not unlike her house; a warm little woman, tucked away in a large close-knit family, full of secret places.

A marvelous storyteller, her eyes light up when she speaks and she becomes the people she's talking about. For years Rachel told her stories to her children, grandchildren, friends, and family in Belgium and America. Everyone told her she ought to write her history, to pass on to her children.

Rachel and her husband, Lud, finally took that advice and began struggling to piece her stories together. She compiled a good deal of information from Belgium, letters and photographs, while Lud diligently attended memoir-writing classes. Each story was in itself interesting, but collectively it was a writer's dream or nightmare, whichever way you want to look at it. So many strange and scattered events tossed her around during the first twenty years of her life. Not even her closest family members knew the various details or how all of these stories fit together. In time, Rachel and Lud found putting the story down more difficult than they thought.

I was working my way through college when I met her again. Knowing I was a writer, Rachel told me about her project. She didn't know anything about writing, and she asked me to take a look at the materials she had. I was startled by how unusual and dramatic her story was. Although she tells it simply, this was not the simple story of a happy, upbeat elderly woman whom I had met years ago, but a terribly complex narrative about a tiny town in a small country and a large Catholic working-class family torn apart by politics and prejudice, turned on its head and trampled over by circumstances beyond its control, and how all of those pieces trickled down to the simple life of a young child and forced her to grow up before her time.

It was a daunting task. I must confess, I wasn't convinced I could do this kind of story, but I agreed to put together three chapters to see what happened. We met once a week for about a month, and we sat across from each other. I asked questions, and she started talking. My eyes bugged out when she started telling me her stories in her own words. She speaks with a strong Flemish dialect, and her English is far from perfect, but her honesty, sense of humor, and manner of speaking outright convinced me that all I really needed to do was write down exactly what she said. She loves to talk and I love to listen, so we clicked right away.

I couldn't stop at three chapters. We met every week for three years, I taped our conversations, and after we were done, I transcribed the tape. I didn't try to change what she said or the way she said it; I didn't remove the bits that were not grammatically correct. She uses the English language like a jungle gym, and that is as much a part of her remarkable personality as her stories.

Many times as we worked together, coming up with events that had occurred more than seventy years ago was more than a little painful or frustrating for her. I had to dig deeply into her memories, and there were times I felt genuinely bad about it. Often, she laughed or openly wept. Sometimes I think you will hear her chuckling or weeping as you read her words. As painful and as personal as it was at times, we became very good friends. But keep in mind these are her words, her expressions, her accounts, and her opinions. Lud sat in on most of our sessions, and he helped fill in some details when he could, so a few times it is his voice you are hearing.

Rachel is brutally honest. That certainly comes across, though she will often give the disclaimer that it is not the institutions she is talking about, but the people.

We went to great lengths to accurately reconstruct Rachel's experiences in Belgium, and some of her husband's experiences in Indonesia. It's a picture of a real family and a real town and a way of life that has long since passed away, and how those things radically changed over the course of a few years. But it is also a character study. Because of the strong human themes that dominated Rachel's life, I'd like to think that it's a book anyone can read and go away with something, and I know she feels the same.

Daniel Chase
September 23, 2007

CHAPTER ONE

YOU'RE NAILS IN MY COFFIN

WE DIDN'T HAVE MUCH, BELIEVE ME. I HAVE A PICTURE OF ME as a little girl standing in the backyard with my mother, and I'm holding a big round-faced doll. I said, "Where the hell did that doll come from?" I never had a doll in my life. Not even a teddy bear. I think my aunts borrowed it for the picture.

I was born in a home for unwed mothers in the city of Ghent, Belgium, 1930. From what I understand, my mother, Helene, a beautiful young woman of nineteen with almond-colored hair, went to a dance, met somebody on the dance floor, they fooled around, and she got pregnant. In court the guy showed up with his wife and denied that he was the one. So my mother lost, and he went his way.

After I was born, we moved into my grandparents' house in the little Ghent borough of Mariakerke. It was part of a long wall of grayish brick houses next to the canal. When you opened the door, you entered into a little hallway. Past the living room was the salon, where in the evening we played cards, dominoes, or chess for candy, and then a kitchen in the back where we sat around the table and talked and ate next to the coal stove. Upstairs were two rooms, then up more stairs there were one or two rooms. And every house was built the same way.

As a young child, I was always with my grandmother or my grandfather while my mother worked at the weaving mill. I remember standing on a chair and watching horses towing the fat barges down the canal that ran along the cobblestone streets. Once in awhile I went out when my grandmother went shopping, but mostly in the street or not far away.

My mother worked the whole week, then my grandmother took her pay for food. My mother liked to sing and go dancing. On weekends, everybody took a bath and went out. Everybody, except my mother.

My grandmother always had something to say. "You work the whole week, you take care of the kid!" So then my mother rolled my hair and bathed me, and I yelled because it hurt. Then it went around in a circle, my grandmother "poof!" hit my mother, then my mother hit me.

"You should have never been born! You're nails in my coffin!" she said.

I thought, "Oh my God." I was so scared.

On my birthday she brought me a cake and told me, "That's for the nail in my coffin."

So I didn't like that cake too much. But I said, "Thank you, Mother," and I took the cake.

My mother hated my grandmother. My grandmother, Charlotte, was small and stout. I liked her like that. It made her comfortable to me. She always wore a long dress and nice shoes. She had long beautiful black hair, and inside was silvery gray. She was a real strict Catholic, so when my mother and I moved in with them, we were taboo to her.

My grandmother was always praying. She had a big beautiful chair and next to her were all her books. I had a little footstool where I sat by her or I lay on her lap.

She said to me all the time, "There is a right way and there is a wrong way, and you have to figure out what is wrong and what is right."

In the back she cooked. Mornings we ate a muffin and cheese. She made stumpot in the afternoon, a mix of mash potatoes and vegetables with onions, and then put it on toast, and everybody came in to eat. Sometimes she made her own soup, and we ate that with a slice of raisin bread with butter and tea, except on Fridays when we had fish. We didn't have much meat, and the chicken and eggs were expensive. I always liked to lick the pans when she was cooking. When she cooked the milk, I would see that she wasn't looking and steal the top layer of skin with my finger and eat it. She saw me do it, but I didn't know. I was just dumb, you know. She said, "Did you take the skin out of the milk?"

"Nooo," I said.

Then she said to me, "Let me see your forehead!" So I went over to her. I thought she was going to hit me or something. Then she looked at my forehead and said, "You lied to me, because there's a big cross on there!" My grandmother came up with some doozies. She told me, "You know, when you do something just tell the truth, don't lie about it."

I was always scared to death. I said, "Yes, yes, Moo Moo." So I never lied.

When a Catholic funeral went by on horses, you would see a cross on this coffin. Then you had to stop and make a cross, my grandmother said. One time there was a funeral carriage passing by. She stopped, but she didn't make a cross.

I asked her, "Why didn't you make a cross?"

She said, "He doesn't have the cross of Jesus. That means, he goes to hell."

As a child I thought, "My goodness, you go to hell when you don't have a cross on your coffin?"

She was always sitting next to me reading her Missal. She went to Maria, Joseph, the Holy this and the Holy that, but she never went to Jesus or God. On Friday or Saturday my grandmother would go to the church to the guy in the box there. What the hell she did, I don't know, but she went in so often I thought, "She has to be a bad woman!" She had to do five of these and five of these, and I had to sit there waiting until the crucifixion was over, you know.

My grandmother was a funny lady. She hated doctors. She made all the medicine herself. She grew everything in the yard. She said, "Drink it! Eat it!" She had a golden snuffbox with her name on it, and she opened it and sniffed all the time, and I hated it.

I asked her, "Why do you do that?"

"Come here!" she said to me. Then she put my nose in the snuffbox, and I sneezed and sneezed. She was something else.

My cousins, none of them liked her. They called her a witch, because she knew everything. I don't know how she knew it, and I didn't care.

The last few weeks in August we had beautiful weather. That's the only two months you see the sun, believe me. The rest was horrible ice and fog. In the summer we sat outside, and the neighbors waved to us. Every move you made, they knew. Everything you said, they knew. And they came back to my grandmother and said, "Do you know what that bastard Rachel did?"

Oh, they loved that. But that was the only entertainment they got. Some of them had a radio, but that was a luxury. The rest was always, "he said so, and she said so, his wife had a baby, his wife died, he's got a cold and he didn't come to work," stupid lousy things that we don't even think about now. But then that was important. News just traveled through the streets from mouth to mouth. And they lied, you know. "He is sneaking out on his wife and his wife don't know," and it goes on like that over and over. Then in the evening before you sat down at the table, my grandmother said, "Oh! Don't sit down! I have to talk to you first!" Then you have to listen to her stories.

"So-and-so said that you said this and that!"

"I didn't say that!"

"Yes you did!" And whatever they said, she liked it, and that was it. You could say no till kingdom come, but she still believed what they said.

My grandmother was strict with me, but I loved her. She taught me to crochet the curtains, knit, and mend socks.

My grandfather was different. He was tall and slender, had a mustache, and was always puffing on a pipe. I loved my grandfather dearly. Wherever he was, I was like a dog following him around. When my mother and grandmother started in, my grandfather winked at me and got me out of the house. He had a big garden of vegetables, beans, tomatoes, and carrots, and he said, "Pick some beans." Or he sent me out in the front, and he asked me, "Do you want money?"

I said, "Yeah!" Then I could buy some chocolate.

In my time the milkman came with a horse, and the vegetable guy came with a horse. So my grandfather said to me, "Okay, pick all the horse shit up, then I give you a franc."

I would do anything for chocolate.

My mother and my grandfather were fantastic together. The Flemish side was more to the German's way of thinking. They talked, they joked, and they sang. Yeah, they sang a lot, but not nice songs. Dirty songs about the nuns.

What I learned from my mother was not too many good things, I tell you that. When I was sitting down, she always thought of something else for me to do just to make me disappear. She might not love me, but I loved her. I don't know why. Because I was her daughter, I guess.

CHAPTER TWO

SNOW WHITE, CINDERELLA, AND ME

I'M GOING TO TELL YOU A STRANGE STORY. IN THE HALLWAY that led through to the kitchen was a big old-fashioned mirror, like the one in Snow White. My grandmother always told me, "When you look in the mirror, that means you are vain." When I was little I used to stand on a big chair in front of the mirror and do my hair and make faces. But one time I was standing alone in the hallway when suddenly, from behind, something slapped me hard. At first I thought it was my grandmother. I cried in pain and turned around. The hall was empty. Behind me was the kitchen. I would've seen something in the mirror's reflection if someone had been there. But there was nothing. To this day, I never knew who did that. Boy, was I scared. I always thought that evil was in the mirror. And I never looked in a dumb mirror again.

I didn't have any friends, except my cousin, Nathalie. Nathalie lived on the same street and we were always together. She was roly-poly, blonde with dark eyes like her father. She read a lot and sang with her mother all the old German songs. She was scared of my grandmother. Nobody liked my grandmother.

Snow White came in 1938. I couldn't go to movies, because we didn't have the money. So Nathalie cried by her father, "Oh, I want Rachel with me! I want Rachel with me!"

My uncle Edmond said, "Hey, that's expensive."

Nathalie said, "Take it out of my piggy bank!" So they did. For the first time in my life I saw a real movie about Snow White. I cried the whole time. I wanted so badly to be her. And everybody called me Snow White after that.

My other cousin, Florence, was three years older than Nathalie. Florence was okay with me when the parents weren't around. One time, the whole family was together. Me, Nathalie, and Florence were never allowed to stay with the family when they were talking. So we went upstairs.

Nathalie said, "Rachel, it's cold!"

It was cold. I said, "What we going to do? We don't have blankets, they're talking, and we can't go back downstairs."

Then I saw all the Piccolos. My mother was crazy about Piccolos. Piccolos was a magazine from America. It had pictures of all the movie stars, models, and stories from New York and Hollywood, big things. My mother got a bunch of them. She kept them in a big stack upstairs.

I said, "I know what we're going to do. She's already read those." So I ripped them up and we made a big fire.

I didn't like to lie, so when they asked, "Who did that?" I said, "Well, I did."

Oh my goodness. My mother was after me with a big stick she did the laundry with. I couldn't sit for a week. But I didn't care. I was cold.

My grandmother had six children, three boys and three girls. Fredric was the oldest. After him came Edmond, my mother, Michiel, Jenny, and then Sofie, the youngest.

Edmond, Nathalie's father, was always a happy person. He was in his early thirties, had black hair and smoked smelly expensive cigarettes. But he was neat, dressed in beautiful pants, shirts, and always a necktie. He sang good with my mother, and wherever he went, he whistled. Even on the bicycle I heard his whistle so I knew he was coming. He had a tandem for two and he and my aunt went to the coast and back. He liked to ride around with her. He was a painter; inside, mostly doors and walls. They had beautiful fireplaces and he painted these to look like marble. They had money and a beautiful house. My aunt Sarah was from a real rich family that owned a factory for coal. She kept her house as clean as a whistle. Maybe once in a month they went to a movie, but most of the time they stayed at home.

Edmond talked to me, but never touched me. Every spring he called me, and we did things in the backyard together, like beans picking or tomatoes picking. Every morning they brought me cocoa that they saved for me. When I heard my uncle whistle, I flew down, opened the door, and the cocoa came in. Then we sat there and ate.

I liked my uncle Michiel the most, my mother's youngest brother. He was so sweet, tall with dark hair. Michiel was more into sports. He loved soccer. But he broke his hip and he couldn't play after that. Sometimes they bowled in the street. It's like a big black cheese ball and they rolled it with a stick. I have no idea what the hell they rolled it at.

He was in the military, and I always helped him press his uniform. That was when he was young, in his early twenties. Every year the soldiers in Belgium went in for six weeks of training. I didn't want him to go. I hated him that he was leaving. So I took his uniform, rolled it up, and hid it behind the stove.

They didn't call me by name. They just called me "Kleine." I was "the little one." When Michiel looked around in his attic, he called me: "Kleine, what did you do with my coat? Kleine, what did you do with that?"

I said, "Oh, I know where it is, but I'm not going to tell you."

We had a big coat hanger on the door. He grabbed me and hung me on the coat hanger with the clothes and said, "Tell me, or you're going to stay up there."

I said, "I don't want you to go!" and I start crying. "I don't want you to go to Brussels to the soldiers!"

He said, "I have to or they're going to kill me. Are you going to make Michiel come back with no head on his shoulders?"

I said, "No."

"Okay, where is it?" So he took me down from the coat hanger and he kissed me.

He liked to eat crustaceans; muscles, crab, a lot of seafood. A wagon came from the ocean, and you could hear them coming. He always asked me to join him. I didn't want to. He said, "Eat it! Eat it!"

When he got married, I was so jealous of his wife. But I loved her. Her name was Amandine. She would sneak and do things for me. She asked me, "Do you want to clean the cinema with me?"

I said, "Yes."

The boss didn't look at your age. He gave you a sack of money right there. Amandine stood up in the balcony and yelled, "Kleine! Don't forget this! And don't forget that!" She made sure that I did a good job. Then we would find some money in the seats. She didn't say nothing. She put it in her pocket. She was funny, the way she talked and the way she made jokes. But you would never understand what we said, because we killed the Flemish language.

My mother's youngest sister Sofie was a real gentle person. She always mothered me. She made me big pots of medicine, and I had to take baths. But she was not a very easy-going person. Once in awhile she got real pissed off at certain things. My mother told her, "Stand here. Do this and this," and she flared up: "No! No!"

I remember she made a big pot of medicine, and I said, "I don't want to drink that."

She said, "You drink that!" We got in a big fight, and she slapped my hand. She got married just before the war to Lionel. I don't know much about him. They had two boys. I'm not sure, but I think she was pregnant before they got married. I don't think Sofie was ready to be a wife.

My other aunt, Jenny, the middle girl, trained to become a nun. She wanted to be a favorite of her mother's. She stayed in the house, in the front room, just to stay with her mother. But it never worked out. I don't think my grandmother had any favorites.

Once Jenny had five francs. It was fake, misprinted or something, and she couldn't give it out. She said to me, "I have something for you. When you do the dishes for me, I give you five francs." She didn't tell me it was not good money. I was so happy. I did the dishes, nice and clean, in good spirits. Then she gave me the five francs.

The first thing in my mind was, "Oh, I got money for chocolate!"

Here in America you have a doughnut with coffee, but it is not the same in Europe. They go to the store and they have a little tiny cup of coffee and they ask for a praline with it. The real French praline is bigger than the ones in the boxes and not cheap. But it is delicious.

I went to the store. They had all the pralines laid out, and they are all different fillings; one is coconut, the other is oranges, the other is vanilla. You can get some too with licorice on it. You could choose what you wanted, and they put it in little bags for you. A franc bought a big piece of chocolate.

The lady said, "Did you know you have five francs?"

I said, "Yeah! I did the dishes!" I told everybody, you know.
She said, "Oh, you can have this, and this, and this."
I thought, "Oh my God." I came home loaded with candy.
Jenny saw me coming and said, "Where did you go?"
I said, "I spent your five francs."
"Where?"
"Over the railroad."
"Did you?" she asked.
I said, "Yeah! And the lady said I could have this and this. I got a whole bunch of candy, for a whole week." So I went home and put it away.

Later, Jenny told my grandmother, "You know what? I give to Kleine a fake five franc. The lady didn't see it was false."

I was hurt. I thought, "Why did she do that?"

The whole family were pranksters. To them anything is funny. If you dropped dead, they would step over you and say, "Hah, hah! Look at this! It's dead!" That's the way they are, because I don't think they had brains.

To become a nun, Jenny trained for a year. She had to pay for it, too. She was close to finishing. But just before Easter, the Catholics go on a long fast. Then my uncles and aunts dressed up for the Mardi Gras. They went out, the guys one way, the girls one way, and finally they wound up together again. My mother was introduced to Alfred Caluwaerts, a drummer in a marching band, at the Mardi Gras dance, and Jenny went off and met my uncle Erwin. That was the end of the nun business. The church was not happy. I never saw her go back.

Erwin looked real young in his face. He was a clown. He always messed around with you, and you thought he was normal, but he wasn't. He was real tall and skinny, and he never came out without a damn cap on his head. Even when he was in his pajamas he wore the dumb cap. I said, "He sleeps with that thing, too?" He smoked big cigars. He called them "spurts." In our language, a "spurt" is the leg of a stool. He came up with some stupid things.

I wanted so bad a bicycle, because everybody had one. Erwin said, "Humph! I have one for you." So he cut a picture of a bicycle out of the newspaper and put it on my bed.

In the morning I said to him, "What does that mean?"

He said, "That's your bicycle. You just think about it and ride it."

One time there was a girl and she left her bicycle in the street. Erwin said, "Get on it and I'll push you!"

I got on and I started riding it. He left me, and I went "Voom!" right into the canal. Then he laughed and laughed. My grandmother was so pissed off. She lifted her skirt and kicked him. They had to take me out, because I couldn't swim. The water was horrible, because of all the lousy boats, and I drank it. I got so sick I thought I was going to die. They got me shots in my stomach. I was out for a long time. When I opened my eyes, all I saw were two nuns with the white things on their heads, and I thought, "Oh, I must be in heaven!"

Erwin was a homebody, too, and he liked his kids. They didn't have much money to spend outside the door, because everything went to the house. But I never saw him work until the Germans came.

The oldest, Fredric, Florence's father, was well-to-do. He was a nice guy, but stricter to me. He was more stern, like a father. When something went wrong, he took care of it. He did not have too much of a sense of humor.

Fredric's wife's name was Marie. Every year there is a big celebration for the Holy Virgin Marie. Every year, I went and bought something for her with my last few francs. One time I bought something and took it over to her house. She had a whole big beautiful hallway, and her house was always elegant. She had a lot of people over, and they heard me come in. She said, "Oh, it's you! You know, do you mind? Don't come in, because your feet are dirty."

I said, "Well, I have a gift for you."

"Oh," she said, "Put it on the floor and go away. I'll pick it up."

So I left. But I didn't think nothing about that. That was normal to me. They loved me, but when it came to the house and company, they were embarrassed when they had to explain who I was. But there was a division between the poor and the rich. Florence's family was dressed to kill, and I was dressed like Cinderella.

They always called me Snow White. I was glad to hear that. But then they said that was not a compliment. I thought, "Why not?"

They would say, "Come over," and I cleaned their houses. I always did things for people, so I always looked filthy.

Florence said, "Well, because that's the way it is."

CHAPTER THREE

IS IT LIKE HEAVEN?

GHENT IS A SLEEPING TOWN. THE WHOLE LIFESTYLE IS DIFFER-
ent. When I was young, I slept between my mother and my aunt
in the middle of the bed. The summers were very hot and humid,
and in those days deodorant didn't exist in Belgium. Those two
stunk under the arms. Oh my God, and they never shaved them,
either. In town, you smelled the people on streetcars when they
reached up to hold on. Later I said one thing was for sure: I don't
want hair on my body. Not under my arms, not on my legs, not
nowhere. Because my whole life I smelled that smell, and I never
forgot it. I remember you couldn't take a bath until Friday, and
then everybody went to the bathhouse on Friday night. You got
a ticket, you got a number, and you waited your turn. If you were
a little long in the shower, "boom, boom, boom!" they pounded
on the door. If you left for the bathhouse around 6:30, you got
back around 8 o'clock. By then you stank again. The soap was
lousy brown soap, and it burned. But I didn't care. I was poor,
but I was clean.

The streets in Ghent were small. Cars were only for the rich people. They were the old open kind with the big wheels, and the owners loved them. They drove real slow through town and waved, so everybody saw them. The first car in Ghent was owned by Mr. Meseur. He lived down the street from us. My grandmother gave me vegetables for their rabbits, and I always passed by from school, knocked on the door, and gave Mrs. Meseur the rabbit food. I remember her driving around in the cold with her shawl on her head.

In our town, standing in the street, you could smell the coal and wood smoke from hundreds of stoves waging an eternal battle against the rain and ice. On the corner was an old Spanish castle and three towers overlooking the town that were used for torture in the old times. The castle gave me the creeps. It was real dark and cold in there, and you saw all the torture tools.

Most of the pricey stores in Belgium were owned by Jews, the jewelry and the fur. I don't know where they got the money from, but they had money. Not all of them were rich, but most of them were real smart, because they were always doing things that we didn't, reading books or writing, and they were always working. The stores in Ghent were all privately owned. First you had always the bakery and the groceries, and then the butcher. Each one is closed at a different day in the week: the butcher every Monday, the bakery on Sunday. Sometimes everything is closed.

The baker came on a three-wheeled bicycle and stopped at every house taking orders. Everybody knew each other there, and they asked, "Hey, Charlotte! How much bread today?" And my grandmother checked. The bakery was owned by a lady named Alena. One time I was walking by her house. She had a car and her son and some other kids were playing around in it. Every time the door opened, it hit a lamppost. Stupid me, I passed by and slammed the door on his fingers. Alena came out and smacked me. It scared the hell out of me. She never forgave me for that. Every time she saw me, she said, "Remember his fingers?"

I said, "Yes, I remember."

The milk boy had a horse and buggy they used for weddings and confirmations. My grandmother always took the milk can, and he put a liter in it. The milk was not delivered ready to drink. We had to cook it first. The milk boy was crazy for me, and my grandmother knew it. He always called me, and he gave me candy. My grandmother said, "Unh unh. Come here. I'll take the milk."

His mother was by him sometimes, and she said, "I'll do the milk." Then he looked for me. My grandmother was after me like a horse. Any guy that looked at me, my grandmother closed in. If she caught me, she slapped me. Mostly it was not my fault, because I talked to anybody. She was pissed off with that, too. She stood with her hands in her big pockets and watched me. That meant trouble.

The butcher was over the railroad. I went with my grandmother and when he saw me he said, "What'd you want from me? Sausage? Lunch meat? Or bloodworst?" Bloodworst is lunchmeat, and it is made out of blood. Sometimes they mixed it with tongue and they eat it with applesauce.

I said, "Anything. Just get me something good."

So he said, "Okay," and he got me a piece of Pâté. Pâté is a mix of all kinds of stuff, and it's so good.

There was one big department store they called the Volk where we bought the clothes and this and that. But that was special. My grandmother went once a month there. I didn't care for clothes. I went by the chocolate. My grandmother said, "Come here."

For shoes, every size bigger was more expensive. When my mother bought me shoes, she said, "Put your toes in." She made me squeeze my feet into a tiny pair of shoes. I was walking with my toes curled under.

On my way to school, my grandfather said, "What are you walking so funny for?"

I said, "Oh, my feet hurt!" We stopped and he had me take off my shoes. My feet were blistered and my toes were all crunched up.

He said to me, "I'm sick and tired of your mother! I'm going to get your shoes!" So he took me to the store. I loved to go with my grandfather. He bought me beautiful new shoes. Like sandals, not expensive, but normal black leather walk shoes. White was really expensive, and we couldn't clean it too good.

My grandmother got boots for me that went all the way to the knees. She always told me, "You're going to have nice legs when you grow up."

When I was young most of the people worked at the cotton-weaving factory. The Congo belonged to Belgium, and cotton came from the Congo. There was always a guy sitting in the store. Every time we went there, my grandmother took all her little money and gave it to him, and he said, "Thank you." That went out to the kids in the Congo. That's what he told us. When I see the Congo, it didn't go too far, I tell you. I think it went to the fatsos there.

The churches mostly were in the big towns. Almost every block has a church. The country churches were surrounded by graves, but in town they had trees and nice things.

When you step foot in the church, the whole place smells like myrrh and candles. I loved it. All the gold work, the woodwork, it's beautiful, and the ceilings are vast. I don't know who built the churches, but those people were fantastic. There was a balcony in the back with a big pipe organ where the nuns sang for the choir. The floors were marble, black and white squares. Before Easter was Lent, when the hanging linens were always purple, almost dark. As soon as Easter came, the linens were white, gold, and silver, and the sun came in through the stained glass windows and shimmered against all that crystal. All of the churches had stained glass with pictures of Maria and Joseph, and Jesus in the front going up to heaven, and then you see a crowd. The walls were lined with a beautiful series of paintings depicting the whole story of Christ from the birth to the ascension. You go down one side with the rosary. You stop at each picture, say a prayer, move to the next one, say a prayer, then in the middle you stop at the cross, and then you go back down the other side. You do that special. Like one day if you don't feel good. I did it when nobody was there. I didn't want nobody to see me walking along there.

Most of my family didn't like to go to the church. My grandfather went on Sunday because my grandmother wanted him to. But he didn't overdo it. My uncles didn't go every Sunday like my grandmother did. Forget that. When they went to church, it was only for a holy occasion, like Easter. Then the table was set for a big dinner. My uncle said, "Oh, what're we eating today?"

My grandmother said, "We go to the church first. Then we eat."

So they went with her. My uncles sat in back of my grandfather and grandmother. My grandfather was all dressed up and had a bowler hat on. The guys started blowing on his neck. Every time they did, my grandfather pulled up his shirt collar. Finally he turned around and said, "I think there is something open in here. There's a draft on my neck." The guys just laughed and as soon as he turned around they started blowing on his neck again. When they got home, my grandfather said to my grandmother, "I'm never going to go to that church again! The wind was blowing on my neck! I was so sad! Somebody's window was open!" The guys just cracked up laughing.

My grandmother said, "Ah! That's all your imagination! There are no windows in the church!"

The guys said, "Yes, there was. We got cold, too." They were lying, you know. "Next time we're not going." They did funny stuff all the time to get out of church. But she made them go anyway.

I was always with my grandmother when I went in the church. We came in on our tiptoes. There's a shell of holy water. I put my fingers in there, because I had to be clean to get inside, and sometimes there was a little sponge. When I was little, my grandmother took the water and made a cross for me. Then we tiptoed inside. You can't even clear your throat. If you make noise, boy, the whole church is looking at you. Oh, they'd kick your ass then. "Don't bother me, I'm praying!" you know.

My grandmother always told me, "You go first to Maria. Then Joseph. And then you go to Jesus."

I told my grandmother, "What did Maria and Joseph do? I learned Jesus died for me."

My grandmother said, "No, you can't. You have to go through Maria." But I didn't care for Maria and Joseph so much. We fought over that. My grandmother told me, "I'm going to hit you if you don't listen to me." But, to me, something told me that was wrong.

We crept to the chairs. Then we had to turn our chairs around real quiet, sit on our knees, and put our hands up on the back of the chair. No one talked in the church. The people sat like wax statues. When he preached, we turned our chairs around and sat down. When he finished, we got down, turned our chair around, and went back on our dumb knees again. The people went fast, because they got real good at it. I heard, "Tock! Tock! Tock! Tock!" all the chairs going around, back and forth. My legs were dead by the time I got out of there.

After we sat down, they gave us communion, when they shared with us, "This is my flesh, this is my blood." But we didn't have the blood. We always had that little white thing, but the wine there was too expensive. We had our communion before we went to High Mass.

My grandmother made sure I sat through the whole ceremony. She always pinched me on the butt. She told me before,
"Don't move, because I'm going to pinch you, or I take your ear
off." If I started tapping my feet, that was it. She said, "Look forward before I pinch your ear."

I said, "Okay."

I loved to look around. I liked to watch the organ behind me
with all the nuns singing. In mass, the women had to wear hats.
There were strange hats, too, with feathers. My mother got one
with the veil for her face. I got to staring at all the funny looking
people. And there were funny people, I tell you. I liked snooping around at the clothes. They wore long dresses, black or gray
coats, and smelly cheap cologne from Germany. I always won-
dered, "Who is this lady, who is this?" I thought, "Oh, I want to
be like her." Maybe she was the biggest creep you ever saw, but
it was the way she dressed or the jewelry she wore. My grandmother told me when they had jewelry, they had money.

In the front is a big beautiful stage with Christ in the middle. The priest walks in. He goes from one side to the other, and
comes back in the middle. Then he goes on his knees, he goes
up, he makes a cross, and somebody would sprinkle incense all
around. Then he walks up to the pulpit, takes communion, and
he turns around and blesses everybody. He had real wine, of
course. That was expensive wine, by the way. I could smell it on
his breath.

The priest spoke Latin. We had some songs in Latin, but not
much. He said something in Latin and we answered, "Amen!"
But I didn't know what the hell he was saying. So we said,
"Amen!" to what? He could've said, "Drop dead." We said,
"Amen!" Everything was Latin, except when he went up in the
pulpit and he talked to the people. When he was done with
everything, he prayed, Joseph once, and Maria so. It goes on for
an hour, believe me.

When he preached, he had the Bible by him; a big, big book, and he goes through it, but we don't. We had the Missal. A Missal is like a Bible, but Catholic. They will take little stuff out of the Bible and make some kind of guideline for us; how to be and to live, and that sort of thing, but the Bible was not allowed to us.

We heard, "K-Boom!" a book on the floor from someone who fell asleep. My grandfather was one of them. My grandmother jabbed him in the side with her elbow, and his hat fell off. He had to grab his hat and put it back on. Some of them started snoring. We just looked. But we don't say nothing. We just kept our mouth shut. The priest didn't know. He was too far away. When he preached, then he saw. Sometimes he said, "Oh! Now, I don't think my preaching is so good, so people are sleeping!"

My grandmother knew the priest personally. He was really nice. He had a big house with a maid. We called him "Father." But I never called him father because I didn't like it. He came over. My grandmother was known there, and she got her own chairs with velvet that she paid the church for. He wanted money from you to get the wine. So he said, "Hi, Charlotte! How are you doing? And are you listening? Are you praying?"

"Yeah."

He said, "By the way, do you have a good gift for me? Because I need some material for the church."

"Oh!" My grandmother said, "Sure!" She always had a big belt and under there was her money. She said, "Here."

He said, "Thank you very much, Charlotte." Then he would take off again and go to another house that he knew he would get money for his wine.

On Sunday afternoon we came from church and sometimes ate at home. But there was a pub next to the church. I went in there with my uncles and my aunts, and I played billiards. The priest went in there, socialized, and played billiards for cheese balls. He drank, too. And he could lift them, boy. Nothing wrong with that. They liked it.

They had beautiful Christmas ceremonies there at the church. Santa Claus in Belgium is December the first. Every year Saint Nicholas came with the boat from Spain with Black Peter next to him. Saint Nicholas is all dressed up like the pope. He's got the same hat on, with the cross on it, and he has a long robe, and staff, and everything else. There is a story that we were told. Saint Nicholas found a bunch of kids in the boonies somewhere in Europe. He was a holy man, a priest or something. He got them food, he got them clothes, he picked them back up, and then he brought them to wherever they had to go, school or something.

They go down the street, and the kids they didn't like, they called out. He was so holy, but his helper did the filthy work. He had a whip and whipped the bad children on the butt. He whipped the "mm" out of me, you know. And I cried, I was so scared. I never wanted to see Santa Claus again. The presents were brought by Santa Claus, but mostly candies and chocolates. For the meal at Christmas we had pheasant or rabbit. Sometimes we got a big beautiful roast. I liked that the best.

Then we went to the church and sang. The tree is there, and the stall, everything was Jesus, and I saw all the angels. At midnight, all the bells would ring. Then I cried, because I felt so awful. I thought I was never going to make it to heaven.

CHAPTER FOUR

LET THE ONE WHO HAS SIN WORK

WE ALWAYS HAD TROUBLES. IT WAS A SMALL TOWN, BELIEVE ME. You could drive around the whole thing in less than an hour. My grandmother, or the neighbor's grandmother, or whoever it was, stood outside in the morning talking to each other like nothing else, and they looked at me, at my face, my clothes, my shoes, and then they turned around and whispered in each other's ears. The older people was the worst. I always thought to myself, "Why do they do that?"

They asked, "Where's your daddy?"

I said, "I don't have a daddy." That was it. I was doomed instantly.

I wore the same dress for weeks on end, and that probably didn't help much either. It was the only one I had, and I had to wash it, dry it, iron it on the stove, and wear it again. Doing the wash was hard work. We put the water in a tub, and then the soap, and we scrubbed it with our hands. On the top is a roller

23

that we wrung out the clothes with. They went into a tub of water with soap, then back out of the soap, through the wringer again, back in the pure water, and then we hung all the laundry up on the line.

At my grandmother's house, most of the time my aunts Jenny and Sofie were like the Queens of Sheba, because my mother was the fallen lady. When my grandmother asked my aunts, "Do the wash. Iron this," they said, "Why? Let Helene do that!"

My grandmother said, "Okay." It was like, "Let the one who has sin work."

So my mother did it. I hated that, too. She just came from ten hours work. Sometimes I helped her, and Jenny and Sofie sat with my grandmother and they enjoyed it. My mother would be so pissed off, she said, "At least hang the wash up!" But they wouldn't do that either. So she came in, slapped them with the wash, and made them hang it up. If I knew the Bible then, I would've clobbered them with it. When it came to work, they were so lazy.

At eight o'clock in the morning my uncle brought the bicycle and took me to school. It was an all-girls school. They didn't allow boys in at all. The school was a big huge building where the nuns lived. In the back there was a big yard, and there was a chapel, and we had the front where we came in. We were not allowed to go into the monastery. We could see the windows and the big door, but that is forbidden. My God, you go in there, maybe you'd never come out. I didn't trust the nuns, I tell you that.

There were twenty-seven girls in the class. They gave us green and white dresses to put on over our dresses that closed in the back. It was like a prison, you know. We had to take it off in the evening and hang it up before we went home.

After putting on the dress, if it was nice weather we went to the chapel and prayed in there, or if the weather was too cold we prayed in the class, because they didn't want us to dirty the chapel with our feet. The chapel was smaller than the main church.

It was clean and simple, just a beautiful altar with the golden communion cup sitting on it, a little box in the middle where all the gold was locked up at night, and a statue of Jesus standing there with His hand on His heart, and His heart was bleeding. They tell us that is because the people sin too much, and then His heart bleeds.

The nun brought us in there. We had benches in the back, and then she goes to the front. The nun did the rosary, and then we had to do the rosary before we could get out: ten "Marys" and one "Jesus," ten "Marys" and one "Jesus." Every day the people did that. And it didn't help them.

From there we went back outside for gymnastics. That was taught by a teacher, special trained for that by the church, I guess. The teachers were all old and ugly to me, I don't know. Except the nuns; they were young and beautiful. The gymnastics teacher had a white blouse. Her arms were covered up, and she wore black pants all the way to the bottom. What we'd have to do is, we'd come in and march along the building, and then we'd do our arms and legs, and arms and legs, up and down. After that we got some wooden barbells; they looked like barbells, but they were made out of wood. They were not heavy. We could grab them, and we could lift them, and we could turn them around, and that's what we'd have to do. Real simple exercises, because we sat on benches all day in class. When I came out, ai yai yai, that hurts, wow.

After gymnastics we went into the classroom and we learned. Each class was taught by a different nun. They were pretty nuns, too. I always thought, "What the hell are they doing here?"

We had arithmetic for something like an hour there, then reading, history, and geography. Some of the nuns were really friendly and nice. Some of them were not that nice; they wouldn't laugh, and I said something and they looked at me like they wanted to shoot me. They didn't like me. I was different, I told you that.

When you were a bastard they didn't care for you because you were born in sin. So they always picked on you. They told me what to do and I followed the rules. Belgium, they all had their funny faces that I was scared that they would bite me or something. I didn't see too many happy persons in my time.

We had a little privacy screen in the front, and there was a bucket with water in it all the time, for fires or something, or if you didn't feel good and you had to throw up it was there. One of the girls had to go and piss too much, and the nun didn't like it, so she took her behind the screen, lifted up her skirt, and sat her in the cold bucket of water. And it is cold in Europe. We all were scared to death, you know. We were scared to ask to pee. See, there is a time to pee; there is a time in the morning, there is a time in the afternoon, and when the class is over, but you better pee when it is time to pee, and that's it.

Most of the time for punishment there was a chair and you had to sit there in the corner. I did one time for being late for school. And I never did that again, because it is not a nice picture either. Everybody looked at me. I felt so lousy. I had to pray or meditate or whatever I had to do there, and when the nun thought it was time to get me out of there, she said, "Okay, that's enough," and then she let me go back to my bench.

You know, here in America if that happened the parents would go to the principal, the teacher, make a big ballgame about it, but not there. Sometimes maybe the parents came over, but you never heard about that. Nobody would talk about it. They kept their mouth shut, because they knew they would have problems with the church.

We did singing. Old religious songs, about Maria and Joseph, and I don't know. I don't think I was too good at singing either, and I really didn't care for the songs, so I never sang them. But my lips were moving because I was scared she would hit me with the stick.

Then it's time to eat. We went in the cafeteria, and some people got food and some people brought food with them. It was a long table with a lot of chairs. We had only a half hour to eat there. Because I was alone, and I didn't have too much, most of the time they got me lunches from the nuns there. They made the food, and the food was lousy, oh my goodness. Was mash potatoes and gravy and most of the time meatloaf or Spam, and they put so much salt and pepper in the potatoes I couldn't eat them. That was the cheapest thing that they give you. There was no meat, that was for sure, except for the meatloaf, and sometimes they had a big huge roll of sausage and they chopped it in little pieces.

Then I went back and went over writing. I had a pencil and I had a pen and a pot with ink. All the words had to be together when we wrote there, and we had to write exactly on the line. For Christmas and New Year we made up a letter for our parents. I didn't do that because I had no parents, so I made it up for my grandparents. It's like a beautiful "thank you," on special paper, and I said, "Dear Grandparents, this year I did this and that, and I thank you for this and that, and what you gave me." You know, stupid dumb things that nuns make up.

Belgium is two languages, French and Flemish. It depends where you are. The Walloonish side speaks French. They call it the Walloons, because it's not like you say in Paris. It's like a slang. Liège is French, Brussels is French, Antwerp is Flemish. Eindhoven is Flemish. My city, Ghent, is all Flemish. So, because Belgium is split, at school we had to learn the two languages. That was the law. Every time I spoke French, my mother said, "Over my dead body!" Boof! Boof! Boof! "I don't want to hear French in my house! That has nothing to do with you! That's for the rich bitches!"

I said, "Okay! Okay!" So at school, when I hadn't learned my French, the nun hit my fingers with a big stick. I said, "But my mother said not to speak French."

So she said, "Why?"

I said, "I don't know."

The nun said, "Well, I'll find out." So she sent somebody to my mother. When they came back, they sat me all the way in the back of the class, and she said, "Don't open your mouth."

Not too many kids liked me. I tried to be nice, but I was not normal. When you got a father and a mother you is okay.

Aurelie always sat next to me in that class and she couldn't sit still. She always sat weebling in her chair. The nun didn't like that and they told her to sit still.

So Aurelie said, "Okay," so she sat still for a little while, and then there she went again weebling in her chair.

So finally the nun said, "Okay, since you're that hot, come here, I'll cool you off," so she called her and put her on the bucket, too. We thought, "Oh my God, that poor girl." Everybody in the class was looking, stunned. We heard her talk, but we couldn't see with the screen up there. "Now are you cooled off? Put your pants back on." The nun said, "Now you sit down." Aurelie cried though, poor girl. We had more Hitlers than you think, I tell you.

We didn't have too much freedom. We couldn't talk in a class. Only to the nuns we could, then we had to put our finger up first when we wanted to say something. During lunch we could talk real low, but not much. When we talked loud, they had a stick, and they would hit us with the stick. That shut us up. They said, "Eat! No talk!" In Europe when they hit us with a stick we deserved it, and they don't give a shit.

After school most of the time the kids ran home. I walked with Aurelie maybe five minutes, and then she was home; she lived in town, and I was out of town in Mariakerke. I'd have to go much, much farther, over two bridges.

I have a picture of Aurelie sitting there with her glasses on. I liked her; she was a nice girl. Not too many were friendly, because you had to be careful who you took as your friend. They didn't want you as a friend when something don't go right with your family, if your family didn't have money, or your family didn't have a nice house.

One day we were both coming home together. There are two trams running side-by-side, one going and one coming, and they pass real close together. I was before her, and I was walking, and the tram came. I thought she was behind me, and something happened between there. I had a feeling in my mind that maybe her shoe fell off, she stopped and turned around, and she just didn't see the streetcar coming. I was walking and I heard the tram slamming like crazy, and stopped, but it was too late. And I looked and there she was under the tram. When these things hit you, you are gone, so I don't think she felt nothing. And I hated it. I ran away. I was so sick from it; I think I wanted to jump in the water. I cried and I cried.

I went home like ice. That's when I saw Geoffrey Voorst for the first time, a man my uncle Erwin introduced to my mother, standing by the bushes. He was real small, smaller than my mother, with a shiny bald head and little sneaky eyes. When the accident had happened, my mother was close by in a restaurant on the corner with Geoff. A guy went into the restaurant and said, "There was a big accident." My mother knew I went through there on my way home from school. She asked the people, and they said, "Oh, the body is gone." So Geoff dropped my mother off on the bicycle to see if it was me. Maybe she was happy that I was gone.

That night, I just couldn't sleep. I saw that body; constantly that body in the tram. My grandmother made me hot chocolate and some bagels.

The people said, "Well, she was nice. She's gone, so she's gone." For a long time I couldn't get over it.

CHAPTER FIVE

I DO THIS SO YOU CAN HAVE A NAME

IN 1938, DURING THE SPANISH CIVIL WAR, LOTS OF GYPSIES came over from Spain. My grandmother told me not to talk to them. One beautiful gypsy lady walking by the water looked so tired, and she had no clothes. I thought, "Oh my goodness, I should get her inside." So I ran out to her and said, "Do you want to drink something?"

She said, "Mm hm." So I brought her in.

My grandmother hissed, "Why did you bring her in the house? She's filthy!"

I said to my grandmother, "Look, she's hungry and she's thirsty!"

My grandmother always told me, "You feed the people when they're hungry."

So I thought, "Well, I'm going to teach my grandmother the lesson." I got the gypsy lady some water.

My grandmother came back in the kitchen and talked to her and finally said, "Okay, stay for soup."

That night she wanted to read my palm. I was only eight, but she said everything about me was in there. She said I would get married, I would go over big water, and I would have a lot of kids. She said, "You're going to be awful happy, and you're going to be rich."

I said, "Oh, okay."

My grandmother said, "And don't you believe that!"

Caluwaerts, the man my mother met at the Mardi Gras dance, came to my grandmother's house one day, and my grandmother let him in. He looked younger than my mother. That's when he asked me if I would mind that he married my mother.

I had never seen them together. They only saw each other maybe Saturday afternoon or Sunday. Ghent is loaded with cafés where they could dance and drink, or maybe they went to a movie. That was the cheapest they could do.

I said, "Well, I don't mind that you marry my mother. But I can do without it." I told him, "You and her are going to get married whether I say yes or no." And that's what they did.

Not too many men would marry a woman with a kid. Not in Europe. My mother thought, "Well, he has to love me enough to make the sacrifice."

She told me, "I do it only for you, because I really don't care for him. But then you can have a name, and then you can tell everybody you have a father."

I said, "I want to keep my grandfather's name." The guy was not my father. He was a stranger, and I didn't like him. He couldn't talk. He stuttered, and to me it took too long for him to talk. I don't think he cared for me, either. He wanted to marry my mother, but I think he wanted to chop me in pieces and get rid of me. But that was my mother. I had to accept whatever she did. My family didn't do too much. They said she was crazy, and that was the end of it.

They married on a Saturday, because it was their day off. It
was a real cheap wedding in city hall by a clerk. I was not there,
but afterwards they rented a big room and all the family was
together and we had a simple dinner of soup, salad, and potatoes.
Caluwaerts's family was there. One was a cabinetmaker, a real
nice guy. The youngest one, she later died in a German camp,
and one was a policeman. I never saw them again after that.

My mother moved over the canal. It was real close. I could
run over the bridge and was back to my grandmother. It was
a pretty good little house: a family room, a kitchen, two bedrooms, and a little backyard. It was empty when we moved in,
so they got some furniture from Caluwaerts's family; a table and
chairs, two couches, and that's it. The beds were old iron beds,
and, boy, they made noise, I tell you. The mattress was a bag
stuffed with goose feathers, and instantly I sank down into it.
I had to turn it every day, and you need muscles to turn those
things over, believe me.

Caluwaerts took me to school and brought me back sometimes, and after school he said to me, "Wash this, wash that." So
I worked in the house.

People said, "Your name was always Van Meers, and it is
Caluwaerts now. What happened?"

I said, "Well, I don't know, but I think my mother married
another guy." I was just a child. I got confused.

I didn't see Caluwaerts much. He had a job as a night watchman, and he played music on the weekends in the bars or something. He came home whenever he wanted in the evening and
sat there and played drums, read the newspaper.

My mother came home at six o'clock tired, washed herself,
and sat down. She would not do anything when she was tired.
I'm not certain, but I think she had awful arthritis. Arthritis in
Europe is much more severe because of the dampness. I remember her arms and her hands were real bad. In the morning she

left early, and every day she walked over the canal to the big company where she worked.

I cooked, stumpot and coffee. The coffee pot is a big pot with a bag and the coffee stayed there forever. By the time it is evening, the coffee is so strong that your toes go "ding." Most of the time Caluwaerts and my mother talked, what happened today, the people, what the work was all about, and then he talked about his family. Sometimes he went out on his bicycle to his parents and ate there.

Every year there was a Flemish thing called Eiser Bedevaart. It was a big celebration for all the Flemish people who fought for something or other. They didn't like Jews. They didn't like anything that wasn't in their favor. Every year my mother went there and sang all these Flemish songs. She took me in the bus and from there we would go to the ocean. I sat there so long listening to the yelling and screaming. A child doesn't want all the politics. I wanted to go to the ocean. After the whole thing was over, my mother went to the bus and fell asleep.

I never saw an ocean in my life. I thought, "I have to go to that ocean." So I sneaked off the bus and ran, I don't know where. But I came to the ocean. And there were all the people, swimming and playing. I went into the water, and out of the water, and into the water, and out of the water. I don't know what I was doing. Then I saw a whole bunch of policemen looking for me. The bus was ready to go back to Ghent. And my mother really let me know who was the boss. And she was the boss, I tell you. But in my mind I thought, "I don't give a shit." I was so happy I saw the ocean. I didn't care what she did to me.

My mother liked to argue people in their politics. Caluwaerts didn't take too much of that. Later on, the pots and pans were flying around, because my mother didn't give in, and Caluwaerts wanted to be the boss. Caluwaerts accepted it in the end, and he let it go. He didn't touch her, but they had mouth fights.

And they can be ugly, I tell you. You can kill somebody with your tongue.

In the meantime, I was always in the middle of it. If they said something I didn't like, I said something, then my mother said, "Shut up!" So I went in the corner and shut up.

My grandmother didn't interfere there. But I ran to her when something happened I didn't like and hugged her and kissed her. Then she knew there was trouble.

She said, "What's happened now?" So I told her everything. But she could do nothing.

She always told me, "Well, don't worry. Come by me. Come by me." And I did. But I couldn't stay there. I liked it better with my grandmother. It was easier, too.

CHAPTER SIX

GEOFFREY VOORST

I DIDN'T KNOW ANYTHING AS A CHILD. I KNEW GEOFFREY Voorst was a friend of my mother. He hung around the house all the time, always snooping around there on his bicycle. He and Caluwaerts met one time, but Geoff didn't come in when Caluwaerts was there. He waited until Caluwaerts was out. Caluwaerts worked and wouldn't be at home. Geoff picked my mother up after work, and they went bicycling somewhere. I don't know how often my mother went bicycling with Geoff, but sometimes she sent me away and I slept with my cousins.

Geoff didn't talk to me. He might've said, "Hi," but he stayed as far away from me as he could. He didn't work, so he came in any time he wanted. Even when Caluwaerts was there, Caluwaerts thought, "Well, he's just hungry." My mother let him eat.

After awhile, I think Caluwaerts had an idea that she was messing around with Geoff.

My mother was horrible. She said "No!"

He said, "Yes!"

She said, "If you don't like it, there's the door!" She wanted him to go.

Caluwaerts was a nice person; he never hit her. But my mother hit the table or something, and he backed off. I don't think my mother was ever polite to nobody.

I was not a saint, either. I went and told my aunts everything my mother and Geoff were doing. My aunts looked at me, and they said, "Tell me that again." Then they went to my mother and had a big fight with her. I loved that. But remember, what you give out you receive? Well, I did, too. I received a fist when I got back.

My mother said, "Oh, Jenny told me this and this and this."

I said, "Not from me!" Then she came and hit me.

My mother and I didn't get along too good. To me, anything she did was wrong. She would make soup, the same soup my grandmother made. When my grandmother made it, it was heaven, but when my mother made it, I said, "Oh, I hate that soup!" She got so pissed off with me. My mother and I got in big battles. I told her, "Get rid of me. That would be the best thing!"

She always said, "Don't talk! Don't talk!"

I told her, "Kill me!"

She said, "You lousy bastard!" Poof! Poof! Poof! And my head flew around. But I wouldn't shut up. I wish my eyes were bullets. I think she would be dead. She hit me one time so hard, I went deaf in one ear. Nothing was happy for me.

In 1938, after only six months, Caluwaerts took his stuff and left. I never heard of him again. They split until the divorce went through. It took a long time, because the one that lost had to pay the court costs. She had to go to the courthouse, but I was not there when that happened. There you don't divorce that easy, and I always had his lousy name after that. I hated it.

In the church law, I don't think my mother could ever marry again in the church, so after that, my mother just dumped the church. We had to move to a tiny, one-room house in the city. At night, my mother was alone with me in the room, and I always slept with her in the bed. Then Geoff came in and slept with her, and she threw me out on the couch.

One night, when I was on the couch and he was in the bed, the cops came knocking, "tap, tap, tap," on the door. My mother motioned for me to get in the bed, and Geoff went to the couch. I crawled in there. I didn't know what was happening, because I was half asleep.

The cops came in, and they said to my mother, "We have papers on so-and-so from Caluwaerts, because he knows that you're sleeping with so-and-so."

My mother said, "No! I sleep with my daughter. He sleeps there."

The cops said, "Oh, is that so?" Then they said to Geoff, "Come out."

The cops took me out of bed and the one cop went and felt the beds. They said to me, "Where did you sleep?"

I looked into my mother's eyes and they were not good. I thought, "Oh my God, the cops are going to take them away." So I said, "Here."

They said, "No, you didn't. You slept there."

I didn't say nothing. I couldn't lie.

"Aw, no!" said Geoff. "She's lying. She always lies!"

The police said, "No, she's not, because the bed's still warm from your feet. And her feet are only so long." He said. "Little girl, you go sleep with your mother." And they went out, and they knew exactly what happened. When they were gone, I got a beating from my mother.

The people always said, "So the mother, so the daughter."

I thought, "Oh my goodness. I'm not going to be like my mother."

CHAPTER SEVEN

WHEN I HAVE TO DIE, I'LL DIE HERE IN MY BED

IN 1940 GEOFF WAS LIVING WITH MY MOTHER. THE APARTMENT was a dumpy place in the cheap end of town. The room was not much, believe me. Somebody bought a crummy house, set up the rooms with some old furniture, and then rented the rooms out. Everything was in there: a real tiny bed, a little table and chairs, and a potbelly coal stove. We all lived close together at that time. I walked between the apartment, my grandmother, and my uncles.

I didn't know anything about Hitler. The king from Belgium, Leopold III, his family was from the Royal House of Saxe-Coburg and Gotha. Hitler said to Belgium, "Listen, the war is not about you guys. Sign off, and then I won't do anything to you, because you have Germans in your family, and I want to give you a chance. But if you don't we'll take Belgium anyway." I don't remember exactly what happened, but Hitler met the family, took them hostage in a castle in Germany, and he took Belgium.

It was in May, I remember that. There was some shooting or something, and then it was quiet. After that we saw the Germans driving all over the place. They made their headquarters in the castle with the three towers in Ghent. We kept quiet in the house. The people were scared, believe me. I was ten years old, I didn't know them, and I didn't know what was happening. But my mother was happy, so I thought I was happy.

First they took anything that was metal. They took the lanterns down, and everybody had to contribute to the war material. Every house, the Germans came in and asked. My grandmother had to get the copper, the tin, the silver, everything we had in the house. My grandfather cried and cried and cried. Hey, when you worked hard all your life like he did and somebody came into your house and took everything, I don't think that's a nice picture for you. He was just so tired, too, you know. The Germans were not stupid. They looked at us. They saw when we lied. But we did not fight them. We had no weapons.

In the beginning, people disappeared and the stores closed down. We never saw soldiers in the streets. They came in the night. As soon as it was dark, we could not go out no more. The windows were blacked out. We could not light a candle. We could not even smoke or the Germans knocked on the door and said, "We see light." They were toughies. We heard some bombing, too, and we heard shooting, but we couldn't get out. We locked ourselves in the basement of the house.

In my time, Catholics didn't like the Jews. My grandmother said, "They killed Jesus and they are doomed forever." But as a child, I didn't think about that. In school, I knew a girl. She had real long black hair. I can't remember her name now. She lived close to Aurelie's house. Next to the café her father had the barber shop, right by the three towers. We sat next to each other in class, she waited for me, and then we would go to school together.

She was real smart. In class sometimes she would slip me a little note and help me out. In my house when I asked for help, my uncles said, "I don't know. I didn't go to school." One morning, the barber shop was closed. The father wasn't there, and she was not there. On the store was a sign with a picture of the Star of David, and then above it was written in German, "Jew." Later I knew what happened. The Germans went in the night and got them out. Wherever they took them I never saw them again, and in the school, nobody talked about it. The nuns were afraid. I was so pissed off about it, because I loved her dearly. The nun said, "We pray for her."

I thought, "What are we praying for? Is she dead?"

"No," she said.

I asked her, "Where is she?"

The nun said, "We don't know. All we can do is pray for her."

I thought, "That's stupid."

In Belgium, the Jews wore a yellow star. The Germans didn't touch them. There was politics involved, I guess. But they didn't give them food either. They were so hungry they dug through the garbage bins looking for food.

In the war they closed the schools and the churches, too. Hitler wanted to make his own special people, but it was nothing to do with God. They took all the things from the Jews out of the temples, and they had a big bonfire in the middle of the city and they burned all the religious stuff. That didn't happen by me, but I heard it happened in Antwerp in Belgium. When we went to church, we had to be careful, because we could be killed, too, you know. Big masses and big ceremonies was not allowed no more. They couldn't afford it no more either.

The boats in the canal were laid on their side and the Germans cut holes in them, so they couldn't go up and down no more. The Germans came around and told us, "Don't go out. Don't go out." We had food for about a week, fish, bread, whatever. We had to be prepared for that.

Everybody had a bomb shelter. The people that couldn't afford a bomb shelter made one. My grandmother had a bomb shelter in the back that my grandfather and my uncles built. They dug a hole with steps going down into a wooden framework and rebars that was supposed to keep the dirt from falling in. But it was too small to sit down, so we just stood there waiting. The railroad was by us, and the planes bombed the railroad. The neighbor's bomb shelter collapsed when they were inside it, and they died. My grandmother's collapsed, too. Lucky for us, my family was not in it. I just said, "No way am I going in there. I'm scared of these dumb things. When I have to die, I'll die here in my bed." So from then on I just crawled under the table.

A lot of other people died, because some of the bombs missed the railroad and hit a whole bunch of houses. That's what you have in war. But we were happy there was someone bombing the daylights out of the Germans.

I was there at my grandmother's house in the morning. On the other side of the canal sat a line of villas with beautiful trees. The Germans came and told us to stay in the house and not to open the windows in the front. The Germans were across the canal in the villas and in the trees watching us. I don't know why they were there, but I think they were expecting some trouble from the fields in back of the houses.

The neighbor next door worked for Good Year. Every morning he took his bicycle and he rode up to his job. He thought, "I'm a big shot. I'm working for Good Year Tires." He opened the door, and the Germans shot, "Boom!" and there he lay, right there in the doorway. I was in the house by my grandmother when that happened, and we heard yelling and screaming. His wife ran around inside the house, she couldn't close the front door, and she couldn't get out. Every time something moved, the Germans shot at the house. So she crawled out through the window all the way through the back gate to my grandmother's house, shaking and crying. Her kids were there, too, but they don't move. We didn't have a phone, so he lay there all day. Finally, the Red Cross came with the arm patches and white flag and picked up his body. It was a mess, too.

Germany needed the help to go against Russia. They got everything else, but Russia was really hard. They asked, "Who wants to fight?" Volunteers got extra money; extra coupons for bread, for this, for that, and Hitler did deliver. So Geoffrey Voorst joined the S.S. My mother was already in favor of the German system, so she joined, too. She got a woman's uniform, a white blouse with a big red-and-white arm band, an orange tie, and a black skirt, and then she had a big pin that would let her pass through certain parts of the town. My mother had an attitude then. She thought she was Hitler herself, till she found out she was pregnant with twins.

My grandmother and aunts and uncles hated the Germans, so conflict began in the family. My grandmother told me not to listen to my mother, just do what I had to do because "During the Nazis," she said, "it's not good." My mother and grandmother didn't talk during that time. Because my mother was then in uniform, the family was pissed at her, and they didn't allow her to come to the house. They told her, "You should've never done that." But my mother wanted that power. She had a big mouth with my uncles. And that didn't help me either.

My uncles were all called back to the military. All three didn't go in.

Michiel went to Germany. Just before the war, my Uncle Michiel and Aunt Amandine had a daughter, Sandrine. The Germans gave you a choice: "Are you going to work for us voluntarily, or do we make you?" Voluntarily, you got coupons, your kids were taken care of, and you got a paycheck. So Michiel said, "Well, we have nothing here."

Amandine said, "Where you go, I go."

He said, "Okay." So they went together. They worked together in a factory somewhere, I think it was a weavery, and they had one little room together. Sandrine stayed in Ghent with her grandmother on Amandine's side. She was raised by her grandmother, too, and Michiel sent money to support her.

Edmond didn't want to leave Belgium. The Germans said, "What do you want to do?"

He said, "I don't care what you want me to do. Washing dishes, I'll do that. But I'm not leaving my wife and my kid."

So the Germans said, "How about a watchman? But you'll have to get in uniform."

He said, "I don't give a shit. I'll take it."

He was paid for it. So he checked out the bridges, he checked out the big buildings the Germans were in, and protected that. Edmond wasn't really on their side, but there were no other jobs there. Hitler closed everything.

Fredric didn't want to have anything to do with the Germans, so he went to the Resistance. He stayed with his company, mowing grass and corn, making food or something. In the meantime, he smuggled bread and malt. Malt is like a special coffee made from a seed. When he got money, he helped the underground. He made it look like the company laid him off because he was sick. He always had his arm in a sling, and in the nighttime he disappeared. Where he went, I have no idea. We found out later, he had people under the floor in his house. But nobody knew that, because the Germans would've killed them. That's why he didn't want nobody there. My mother couldn't come. I could, but I didn't see Fredric that much.

You never saw the Resistance. In certain towns you heard about it. They would find a German killed. The Germans would go to that place, get all the people out, the men and the boys. First they asked them, "Who killed him?" You don't know, they don't know. The Germans said, "Okay." They came back. They said, "Who did that?" You don't know, they don't know. The third time they asked, and nobody wanted to tell them who that was, the Germans said, "Well, listen, somebody knows something." Then they shot all of them.

I don't know why, when there was lightning and thunder, I was in the room with the pillow on my head, but I was never scared of the bombing. When they said, "Five o'clock, you cannot go out of the house no more," I didn't know what they were doing. I heard, "mmmmm, boom, boom, boom, boom." But I don't know who's there. I always thought it was the Germans, but it was the allied planes.

In Ghent, nobody could go past the German check points. If you tried it, they would shoot you. But when I stuck my mother's special pin on, I could go to the Germans and explain I had to go here or there, and they saw the pin and led me wherever I had to go and took me back to the house. I was not scared, as long as I was wearing that pin.

Fredric had trouble getting food. They put a couple of German guards on the farms, and farmers couldn't farm the land or they would shoot them. There was a lot of black market in Europe and the Germans were afraid the farmers would be giving food to the black market. The Belgians in the Resistance or the Jews who had money, they could go to the farms and buy from the farmers for black market. And some of them were shot, too.

Me and Jenny helped out getting Fredric food. They knew I could use my mother's pin. I stole from my mother the coupons that she got from Germany, and I brought it to Fredric to feed his family. That's why Fredric loved me. He said, "We have stew for you." I ate that stew, and I was happy.

CHAPTER EIGHT

YOU'RE GOING TO MAKE IT THROUGH, BUT NOT WITH ME

ONE DAY HITLER CAME TO GHENT TO MAKE A SPEECH, AND MY mother went to hear it. I had to go with her. He spoke in German. My mother understood, but I didn't. Everybody thinks he was crazy, but I don't think so. He was from Austria, and they are really bright people. He was tall, with a little mustache, and always in uniform. He was not bad looking. He was cold, yes, but friendly, like a father type. But that is the scene he gave you. Maybe behind the scene is a whole different ball game.

At the time of my first confirmation, I had long hair, and my grandfather loved it.

Every night my grandmother cut the newspaper in long strips, brushed table beer into my hair so that it was sticky, and then rolled it up like curlers and fastened a little piece of yarn to hold it. Oh, it hurt. In the morning she took all the papers out, she washed my hair with vinegar, so it was soft, and then

45

she brushed it on a little broomstick and it would hang in big long curls, like candlesticks, and in the front was a big foo foo. I looked awful.

A few days before my confirmation at the Catholic Church, my Aunt Jenny took me out for my seventh birthday, and she had my hair cut. When my grandfather saw that, he wanted to kill her. They had to send me to the basement until he calmed down. I didn't mind, because my hair was always long. Why Jenny did it, I have no idea. She thought she was funny, I guess.

The final confirmation is when you're eleven. Then you're finished. Six weeks before my confirmation, I had to learn the whole catechism. Every morning I went to the church. For the first time, I had to do confession. The priest didn't say too much to me on that. He told me, "You better don't kiss the boys, you better don't kiss the boys."

I said, "I'm not thinking about kissing the boys." I told him, "You're thinking about it, but I don't. I want to go to school."

He said, "Maybe you swore, or maybe you did this." Once in awhile I swore. When I was a little girl I could swear, believe me. I picked it up from my aunts. The priest said, "Okay." Then he got me three or four Marias and one the Father, I think.

As I learned the catechism, I got points. Then I had to take an exam, and if I passed I would get a big, beautiful, white, gold bound Missal. I couldn't buy it. I couldn't afford it. When I passed the exam, I thought, "Oh God, I made it! I made it!"

So then my grandmother said, "Oh, you're going to get your Missal!"

I said, "Yeah, I made all my points!"

She said, "Good."

The first day of the confirmation I dressed in white, and then we went to the church where I did all the classes. My mother was about six months pregnant from Geoff, and you couldn't miss it. She was heavy duty. My grandmother didn't want her in the church. She told my mother, "You don't come near the ceremony. You're a disgrace to the family."

So my mother stood out in the rain looking on while my grandfather and grandmother took me in the church. Then I saw out in the tree somebody waving. It was my mother. I was so upset because she couldn't come inside. I went in the church crying. All the kids were sitting happy, and I was like, "sniff, sniff." And my grandmother said, "Don't cry! Let her alone! Don't cry! Look what she did to you!"

There was a beautiful ceremony where the nuns sang. There were a bunch of bishops in white and red with the dumb things on their heads. The bishop sat in a beautiful chair, like the pope. Then we had to go one by one up to him. He put oil on my head and said something. He folded my hands for me, and then it was all over. And I didn't get my Missal! I cried. I said to my grandmother, "He didn't give me my Missal! He gave it to somebody else!"

So then my grandmother said, "How can that be?"

I said, "I have no idea, but you ask him, because you paid for your chairs and you gave him the wine for the church."

So she did. He came out, and my grandmother asked, "What happened? Why didn't she get the Missal?"

He said, "I had to give it to so-and-so, because she has a father and a mother, and Rachel doesn't."

I cried and cried. No Missal. So later when we left, my grandmother said, "See! Another thing from your mother! It's your mother's fault!" She said, "Because she did something mean and filthy and you don't have it now!"

I stood next to my grandmother at the table, and I felt so sick. I thought to myself, "I learned that much, and I went through six weeks kneeling at the cross, and I don't have the book because I don't have a father!" I told everybody that was the last time I would ever go to that church.

My grandfather was happy I made it. He told me, "Well, don't worry about it. I will buy you one." But it never was. A few months after my confirmation, he fell ill. He was out for a long time, in a coma. In Belgium the doctor came in the morning and in the afternoon, and the priest came every day. Charles, the family doctor, was from Belgium, but I don't know where; dark hair, light skin, and his voice was real gentle. He was a house doctor for the whole town there. What I wanted really was a father, and I think I saw Charles as a father to me. He said to me, "Take good care of Grandma, and hang on Grandma," and I did.

My grandfather was lying in the kitchen on the bed. My aunts came and stayed with my grandmother. My grandmother couldn't handle it. It was a cold winter. I had to go by the railroad and pick up all the coal and wood that I could find there. I came back one evening so tired and I went and slept with my grandmother.

In the night, my aunt came and she told me that my grandfather asked for me. So I went down to the kitchen, and it was like a miracle. He was wide awake. I thought, "Oh my God, what happened?"

He hugged me and talked to me. He said, "I dreamed about you." Then he said, "I'm leaving now. Hang in there, because I know you're going to have an awful cross to bear." But he said, "Just take it. The Lord's going to provide, and you're going to make it through. But not with me." And he hugged me, and he lay down, and he died.

I was broken. I knew when he was gone I would lose everything, and I did. I couldn't sleep no more. I wanted to go with him. I said, "Lord, take me!" But He wouldn't.

My grandmother came down, and she knew she lost something. She don't know what she was losing until it was gone, and then she felt alone.

My mother was not there when my grandfather died, but I think she went in pain just the same. She didn't like her mother, but she loved her father.

My grandfather was everything to me. There was his grave, and every day I ran there and stayed with him and lay with him. I couldn't get up. Finally Charles said I was going to get pneumonia. It was awful cold. So he got me some pills to make me sleep. But I feel that what my grandfather said, I knew that it was going to happen. Every time I had to face a crisis in my life, I remembered what my grandfather told me.

CHAPTER NINE

WHAT ABOUT HER?
WHAT ABOUT MY MOTHER?

BY THE TIME I WAS ELEVEN OR TWELVE, I DIDN'T TRUST THE priest no more. Just for that book alone, the whole church stank to me. I thought, "When you are that sneaky and that prejudiced, who wants it?" But that don't mean I don't believe in God. A verse in my Missal said, "When you don't have a father, I am your father," and that was always in my mind. I said, "Well, I'm going to talk to my father." A church close to my school, with monks in brown, was always open. So I sneaked in there, put a candle on, and I sat real quiet and prayed and talked to God, whatever was on my mind. I think that helped me a lot.

My family didn't like Geoffrey Voorst. He was friends with my Aunt Jenny's husband Erwin from when they were young, but Erwin didn't like that Geoff went to the S.S., so they split up. Geoff was from Holland. His family were Quakers, always dressed in black, and he always talked about the Bible. He said to me, "The Bible says that the father can sleep with the daughter."

I didn't know the Bible. I thought to myself, "What are you telling me for?"

Geoff had two brothers in Ghent. One of his brothers never talked to him and didn't want nothing to do with him. We went over to his house one time, but he was all paralyzed, and then he died. His other brother I met one time, and that was it. He later died, too, in a German camp. Sometimes we saw them on the street, but that was it. Geoff was the only one in the family who was S.S. Well, they were different from him, and nobody wanted him over to the house.

Geoff sat around the room all day smoking, or he rode around on his bicycle. He did drink, and he loved women. He told us a whole bunch of stories that when he was in Poland he raped a woman. He had to be proud of that. And my mother just sat there. I have no idea if she loved him. I don't think my mother loved nothing. She had a bunch of kids with him, but that don't mean anything either.

Geoff looked good in his uniform. Well, everybody looked good in that uniform, and he was into the Hitler thing, and everything was perfect for him then. That's what my mother fell for, I guess. To me it didn't change. I didn't like him from the beginning, and my grandmother didn't like him, either.

If my mother had a glass placed on the table a certain way, or a chair was crooked, a newspaper, some stupid, lousy reason, Geoff started snorting like a pig. Then my mother got scared. He first started swearing at her, called her names, and then he hit her. He tried to hit me, too, but I told him, "If you touch me, you're dead!" Then he got scared and backed off. But when he couldn't do it to me, he took my mother. He knew that would infuriate me.

Geoff and my mother were together for one year before the Germans put him in uniform and took him to Russia. He drove the truck for the Waffen S.S. These S.S. divisions were very large, from infantries and tanks to air force police. Geoff's job was to sit next to a driver in a convoy or something and carry a weapon to protect the driver in case of an attack.

After he left for Russia, I prayed, "Have him shot in Russia. Get the bullet in his head." But he never was. I didn't think I was getting through to God.

The only time I saw Geoff was when he was there on leave. But he didn't stay long. Every time he came back he got some money, and we ate something. One time, he came home from Russia, and it was cold. My mother was messing around with him, and I was in the way. She told me, "You do the cooking."

I said, "I'm cold!" But I listened, because it was my mother. So I made the potatoes and the gravy. The potatoes had to be brushed off outside, because we didn't have a kitchen inside; just the stove, that was it. So I went out and I was pouring out the water, and the lid fell off. The potatoes fell out where they dump the piss pots. But I was so hungry, so I picked up the potatoes. I thought, "I'm not going to say anything," and I put them on the table. I didn't eat them. I looked at Geoff and I thought, "I hope it poisons you." But nothing happened. Then he took off again.

Geoff was in Russia when the two kids came. When my mother went into labor, I ran and got my aunts, and we helped my mother get to the hospital. She had the twins, a boy and a girl. After they were born, my aunts stayed away.

Then my mother ran out of money. She said to me, "Help me."

The whole world changed for me. Every day was a memorable day. You needed money to buy food and rationing coupons for the eggs, for bread, for milk, for fish, whatever it was. We had loads of coupons, but no money. So I went to families who didn't have any rationing coupons and sold the coupons, so we had money to buy the food. Because my mother was pregnant, I stood in line for whatever she wanted, and then went home and fixed it.

My mother said, "Ooh, I need this." Sometimes I didn't have money either. So then I had to go to my aunts and ask them if they had some money for milk, for my sister and my brother or something. My aunts would be pissed. They said to me, "What's wrong with your mother?" So they got me money, and I got some milk.

After my grandfather died, my grandmother was no longer there to help me. It was horrible for her, too, because my Aunt Marie took over. Fredric moved in with her.

We were supposed to be getting money from the S.S. My mother didn't see the money, so I went down with her to the Kommandantur. Then we found out this check that Geoff made out was 75% to him, and 25% was what he left for my mother. I said to the guy, "What about her? What about my mother? That's his wife. See all the kids there? That's his."

The guy said to me, "So what happened?"

I said, "I don't know what happened. The only thing I know what happened is she don't have the money to feed them. So you better do something about it."

Before my mother had always worked and worked and worked, but she changed after the twins. She just sat there at the kitchen table and played solitaire all day. I think she was somewhere on another world or something. She couldn't face it. So I did everything. I took care of the kids, and they were horrible. My mother breastfed them because so long as she kept them breastfed, then they didn't need food. But I had to go out and get food for her.

Every day we needed something, so I got up in the morning, put some clothes on, and went out. I went from door to door asking people for food. Mostly I went to the richest people that had big houses. They didn't know me there, but they were nice to me, and I asked nicely. Some people gave me the potato peels, whatever there was, some people don't. Or they had some old bread that they threw away or something, or they made sandwiches. I carried the stuff in a black bag, and whatever they gave me, I put it in the bag. I went to this street, that street, and when I had enough I said, "Well, I can feed them today," and then I went home and fixed it, washed it and cooked it.

I wrapped the two babies in towels and slept between them, one in each arm, to keep them warm. I lay like a statue. I couldn't turn, because I was scared to hit the kids. I remember laying on the bed between my brother and my sister freezing, thinking: "I never want kids! I never want kids!" We didn't have coal because the war was on. I went to the railroad and picked up whatever coal was left over from the bags of junk. I had fifty kilo of coal on my neck to go to my mother's house. In that time, the railroad had these big timbers. We was not allowed, but, sneaky, when nobody was there I chopped these things, and then I had, at least for a little while, heat in the house, and I could cook on it. Then it was full of tar, so it burned like hell. The stove broke from the heat. But that's the only thing to do.

I was like a toothpick. You should've seen me. We had no milk, just for the kids, and I couldn't touch it. Most people who starved would get sick with diarrhea. I didn't have diarrhea or nothing. I just couldn't go, because there was no food in my stomach. I wanted to sleep. I got up though because I had to save the kids. But I was just a child, and because of the hunger I had a constant awful pain in my stomach. I thought I was going to grow up deformed.

One time Geoff was away, and I was alone with my mother. My brother was just bundled there and he slept. So she wanted to feed him. My sister's name was Sarah. I remember my mother saying, "Sarah, you have to wait till your brother's done." Then she took him, and he didn't respond. He wasn't sick. He just didn't move no more. He slept, and he didn't wake up. Then she started going crazy. She said, "Get me a mirror! Get me a mirror!"

I asked, "Why do you want a mirror?" I thought, "Is she going to look at herself or something?"

She took the mirror and put it next to his mouth. There was no breathing on the mirror, and then she screamed, "Get the doctor! Get the doctor!"

So I went bananas. I thought, "What the hell is going on?"

She said, "Take my pin!"

I took the pin from her. It was after dark, five o'clock, you could not go out no more or they would shoot you. So I went to the Germans and said, "Can I go to the doctor?"

They said, "Okay. Let me see the pin."

I said, "My little brother, I think he is sick," in my language. They understood us.

The German sentry said, "Okay, I'll follow you." So he did.

I went to the doctor, and I told the doctor. The doctor said, "Okay, I'll come right away."

So that German brought me back home, and the other German that was with him, there were always two, brought the doctor home. Then the doctor told my mother the baby was gone. My mother went crazy. She told me, "You didn't take care of him! He died from the cold!" And I was so upset.

The doctor said, "The baby just died because it was a crib death. There's nothing you could've done." So he wrote up the papers, and he said, "Tomorrow I send somebody with a little casket to take him away."

Then my mother told me, "Go to Aunt Sarah and tell her to come here!"

It was an hour's walk. So I had to get the pin again, and then I went over to her house, knocked on the door, and told her everything that happened. She got me something to eat, because I was fainting, and she came back with me with my pin through all the Germans.

In the morning, the doctor sent somebody to pick up the little body. Lucky Sarah was there. My mother didn't want to let the crib go. The doctor said, "You have to let him go. We take him away." She had to pay, because they brought it to the house.

He never had a burial. I think they examined the body to find out what it was, and then they buried it or something. My mother wrote Geoff about it. I never heard anything more, so I don't think he really made a big deal about it.

After my brother died we had to get out of there. We moved in with my Aunt Jenny and her daughter Stéphanie. Stéphanie was older than Sarah. Stéphanie was close to me, because I helped her learn how to walk. She was a late walker, and nobody could make her walk. But one day I called her, "Come here, Stéphanie! Come to me!" And there she walked. Everybody stared amazed and said, "You make miracles working!" She was a real quiet little girl and simple. My Aunt Jenny was like that, and her father Erwin was cute. She had a little bit of both of them.

Two years after the twins were born my mother had another boy, Antoine. He was born in Mariakerke in Jenny's house, in September of 1943. Geoff stayed there on leave for maybe a week, and then he was gone again. When all the kids were born, Geoff was never there. My mother had no doctor, so I had to go and get the lady on the corner, and she helped deliver him. Antoine had a disease on his head, like eczema. My mother didn't want to go, so I had to take him to the hospital.

Again Geoff came back from Russia, and he went for the check. When he came back, we had a fight. He said, "You know where the money went?"

I had no idea, because he took all the money. What he did with it, I don't know. But we only had 25% from the check.

Geoff got that stupid uniform on from the S.S. with a medal (the Germans got a medal for anything), and he thought he was something else. He said, "Now look what I am."

He was nothing in my eyes before, and the uniform didn't do better, either.

I said, "Well, it stinks."

He said, "You better watch out, because I can do anything to you I want."

I asked him, "You know what that uniform means to me?" and I spit on it. I shouldn't have done it.

He blew up to my mother. Nobody spits on a German uniform. He told me, "It's going to cost you."

I said, "You can do whatever you want." In my mind, I never thought he was going to do anything.

They picked me up by my grandmother in the morning. There came two men tapping on the door. They were not in uniform, but they had a plate hanging on the chest that said "Gestapo." Geoff had got papers. I didn't know it at that moment, but he made my mother sign the papers, because they were not married. She was scared from him, so she signed it.

They took me from my grandmother's house to the German headquarters. I sat in the little waiting room. I did know why I was there, and I asked the guy, and he said, "Don't talk."

Then they took me in a room, and they asked me questions. They said, "That is the paper that Geoff has filed against you." It was a little thing, but Geoff made it more.

I said, "Well, I did spit on him. But what he's saying is not true. I didn't say all these things. I just said his uniform 'stinks,' and I spit, and that is the end."

Geoff told them I needed discipline, I was stubborn, I didn't listen to my mother. So the Germans said, "Well, then you'll learn that."

So I said, "Fine."

Right after the questions I was ushered into a room. Then they said, "Well, whatever it is, we have to get you ready because we're going to bring you to Germany."

I asked him, "For what?"

They got me a whole bunch of shots and checked me out. He told me to take my clothes with me, whatever I had on.

I was scared because it was the first time I ever left my mother and my grandmother. It was the first time I was ever alone, and I didn't know what was going to happen, because we didn't know what happened to the Jews. I thought, "Well, it can't be that. I'm not a Jew, I'm not a Jew." But it was no difference to them. When you did something wrong, you were punished. That's the German way. I thought, "Maybe I'll come back in a week." But I didn't.

CHAPTER TEN

I DON'T THINK I'LL SEE YOU BACK IN A MONTH

I'M NOT CERTAIN WHICH MONTH IT WAS, BUT I HAVE A FEELING it was close after my birthday. My mother really didn't have too much reaction to my leaving. She told me one thing: "You're going to go to a camp, and they're going to fix you." She said, "You're too much like your grandfather; you're too much like your grandmother. You're not obeying my orders."

I didn't react much, either. I thought, "Maybe it'll be better for me."

At the station, I remember my grandmother wore a black shawl. She told me, "I don't think I'll see you back in a month. You never know with the Germans. It can take you two weeks. It can take you three weeks. It can take maybe a year." She said, "Whatever happens, whatever they ask you, answer the truth. Don't lie."

I said, "Okay."

My grandmother had been in a prison camp in World War One. She didn't talk too much about that. The German soldiers had intercourse with the women from Belgium, got them pregnant, and then left. All she ever told us was, as the German officers were leaving Belgium she yelled across to them, "You guys are leaving, but the little ones are staying." That's what got her in trouble. But that's all I know.

I got on the train to Brussels. I looked back, and I saw her crying. My mother, she couldn't care less.

It was afternoon when we got to Brussels. Then I saw I was not alone. There were other girls waiting for us at the station. They were all strangers to me. We waited around the station for the train. We sat there, we didn't move, and we didn't say anything. A German man was in charge. When one of the girls wanted to talk, she put her hand up. He asked, "What you want?" She said, "The toilet." Then he followed her. They didn't like us on our own. We don't escape that easy there. If a girl did something wrong, then he yelled at her.

The train came in toward evening, and we all got on. I have no idea when it was, but it was dark. It was an old jalopy train that looked like it was made from wood. It went "boom-ta, boom-ta, boom-ta," like the wheels are going to come off any minute. The train smelled like cow shit, old grass and hay. I have a feeling there were Germans there or something. When they transferred people, there is no bath, so they sweated, they stank, they pooped, and the people smelled. We sat on benches and, boy, it hurt. The train was not big. There are maybe ten wooden seats inside the car, and just one person could pass in the middle. Blackout curtains hung in the windows. We could not open them or they would kill us instantly.

The only guy we saw was the conductor. On the top of his helmet he had a light, like a coal miner. It was dark, and they wanted to see what we were doing. A girl sat with me on the bench. She was a dark, slender girl about my age. She said she had to go to the camp, too. We talked a little bit about it. She said her father was a German officer somewhere. Discipline, everything was discipline.

Sometime during the evening, there was some confusion. The watchmen moved around like they were nervous. The windows were closed so we couldn't see nothing, and the conductor had just a light on. The train screeched to a stop. Then I knew something happened. I thought, "Maybe they bombed the bridge."

The watchman told us to get off the train. It wasn't until we got out we heard the roar of engines. In the sky were thousands of planes. To us, it looked like they were up high. Then we heard, "Boom! Boom!" and the ground shook. There was a river not far away.

The conductor screamed, "On the ground! On the ground!" We fell down lengthwise in a line against a barrier. Bombs came down like whistles. They told us, "Keep those eyes closed!" I couldn't see anything through the dust, but the ground moved, and we heard people screaming and crying; bombing, screaming and screaming, cracking, and the planes. It smelled like hell, and it was burning hot.

I just lay there, dry and scared, and I couldn't talk. I didn't know what was happening. I thought, "God, I'm going to die!" So I cried and cried. Maybe it was ten minutes, but to me it was like the whole dumb evening. I thought, "When are they going to stop?" They went on and on and on. But then I didn't hear bombs no more. The alarms went off, and we heard people screaming and water splashing. A lot of people were burning and jumped in the river. We couldn't look, but we knew there was a lot going on there.

The conductor told us, "Get back in the train!" Lucky for us the damn thing wasn't bombed.

The dark girl lay just before me on the ground like they told her.

The conductor said, "No, leave her alone! Get on the train!"

I cried and screamed, "Take her!" I wouldn't even leave a dog alone there.

He said, "Get on! She stays!"

I looked at her face. Her eyes were still open, and she looked okay to me.

Then he turned her over. Her stomach was burst open and she was bleeding like hell. Apparently she was lying in such a way as when that tremendous explosion spread, the pressure of the blast ripped her open.

At that moment I didn't know. It was, get off the train, get on the train, go. Later I heard what happened. The city was Cologne; the river was the Rhine.

We got back on, and the train rattled off. I was numb. In my mind, I was in another world. I sat confused and crying. I couldn't talk. I couldn't say nothing.

It was a really long trip from Cologne. We came off the train at a little station in Wertach, Germany. It was really pretty, with cows and mountains and everything. It felt like we had traveled to the end of the world.

I thought to myself, "Nobody knows where I am." There were some books and things at the station, and a map lying there. So I looked around, and then I picked the map up real fast, and put it in my dress, so nobody saw, and I kept it.

There were two big oxen, with a wagon there, driven by two boys. One was around eleven years old, dark; dark hair, dark eyes, taller than me, and he spoke with a deep German accent. He didn't take shit from anyone, I tell you that. The other was something else. He was maybe eighteen, tall, skinny, and blond, with a deep Austrian accent. He don't talk to nobody.

There might've been fifteen, sixteen girls, maybe twenty. They got the girls uniforms at the station, a white blouse, gray skirt, with an orange bandana. That way they could see if we ran away or something. They gave me the uniform and took my clothes. All the girls going to that camp piled their clothes on the back of the wagon, and we walked after the oxen.

It was a long walk through a beautiful morning. The road went up and down. It was not hard for me, because I was used to walking. I was scared, really, although I didn't show it. I thought, "I'll never come out of here."

CHAPTER ELEVEN

WHAT THE HELL IS GOING TO HAPPEN TO ME HERE?

WE GOT TO THE CAMP LATE IN THE AFTERNOON. IT WAS A FARM surrounded by rocky mountains with a lot of pine trees, an orchard, and a creek that came down from the snow. I never saw mountains like that before, with snow on them. The mountains smelled like pine, and there was another smell, sweet like an apple. That breeze swept down the valley and felt so good. And outside I saw deer and rabbits with big ears.

The house looked like a candy house. The outside steps were stone and led up to an open wood porch that went all the way around, with chairs and a lot of white and purple flowers. There were gates on both sides that they kept closed at night, and heavy Dutch doors. A big barn sat close behind the house. They had to listen to the animals, I guess.

Before the war, the farm was used as a resort, a hotel with a restaurant and big beautiful kitchens. Now the German soldiers came in a jeep every night to eat, sing, and drink beer.

Mrs. Beckman, the owner of the farm and mother of the two boys that picked us up at Wertach, stood by the door and said "Hi" to us as we came in. She had a nice face, not pretty, but friendly, and she wore an apron.

The house was big and spacious and full of woodwork. Everything was done with carving and hearts. The only stone I saw was the fireplace. My goodness, the fireplaces were big, too. Taller than me. The whole house smelled like constantly they made apple pies and cider and baked bread. I heard sounds of dishes rattling, of cooking and cleaning coming in through the walls. When we called somebody, it echoed down through the house for miles.

The stairs and floors were wood, dark and old, because people always came in with snow on their feet, and the old floorboards and stairs creaked; when we moved, everyone knew where we were going. On the walls were photos of big shots in uniforms, the Kaisers, pictures from Germany, and of Hitler.

The house was split by a big hallway. One half was the restaurant. On that side it was real bright with dancing. We were put on the other side in the same house. Our side was dark and quiet, plain, no pictures, no crosses, nothing. There was no spirit there, like a tomb. We couldn't go anywhere. We better forget about escaping. I don't know if they would shoot us, but I didn't want to find out either. We were so far away from the city, and we had that uniform on, and everyone knew we belonged to that camp.

The first person we met was a big and tall blond, blue-eyed woman named Eulla Heller. Eulla could have been one of the German big shots. She was always in uniform: a gray skirt, black blouse and red tie, gray jacket, a belt, and black boots. She had rank. I don't know what it was, but she wore a big belt across her chest. The others, they didn't have that, so I knew she was high. She had no ring, so I don't think she was married. But people in

Germany seldom wore rings on their fingers, even if they were.
Eulla had a beautiful face and a deep voice. When we don't listen, then her voice goes higher. Her German was really different
to understand. I don't know if she was from Austria or not.

The first night we were all pretty tired from the journey. We
went into a room with a big table that was covered with a cloth,
and Eulla ordered us what to do. She spoke in German, and
there were two Belgium girls there and they explained it to us
in our language. We stood while she went down a list and said,
"You there, you there, you there." Each of us was assigned a chair
and from then on that was our chair. She told us when to sit.
Eulla sat at the end. We sat there and watched while she went
through all the rules, and then Mrs. Beckman brought trays of
food, set them in the middle of the table, and afterwards somebody cleaned it up.

After that, Eulla appointed us our rooms. The bedrooms were
upstairs. There were lots of hallways, I think maybe about ten or
twenty rooms on our side, so there had to be maybe forty rooms
in the whole house. They made sure we were not lost. It was one
stairs up "and you better stick to it." That's what they said.

The room was simple, bare walls, and four double windows,
all hung with blackouts. The bed was a bunk bed, a plain old
wooden bench, and in there was these fluffy blankets full of
feathers that we put over us at night. That first night they showed
us how to make up the bed. We had to fluff it up like a little pillow and fold it at the foot of the bed, and it had to be real nice,
and we had to learn that. But it was not easy, believe me. There's
so many feathers in the damn thing that we had to shake it and
make sure all the feathers go down. There were mice there, too.
But they did nothing to us, because we didn't have nothing. The
toilet was a little pail that we had to take out and clean.

My roommate was from Belgium, and she was meaner than
hell. I don't remember her name. She was taller than me, a little

bit on the heavy side, and had dark hair with blond in it. We all wore our hair the same way, short like the Dutch boy. She had a low voice, and she talked with an accent. It was awful to understand sometimes, because they had a lousy dialect. We don't connect too good, I tell you. We were scared to talk. In the war we had to be careful who we talked to. There could be spies and we'd never know.

Eulla said, "You have to sleep in something German."

I had nothing. So I told her I didn't bring nothing. The kids laughed at me. Eulla looked in their eyes and instantly they were quiet. I couldn't speak German. Eulla understood me, though, but she didn't approve of it. Gusta, one of the teachers from Belgium, was with her. She was a real good-looking person; short, beautiful black curly hair, with a real soft voice. Gusta listened, walked over and told me, "Well, I'll bring you a nightgown." Then Eulla told her something, and then Eulla brought it to me. It was an old jalopy thing that went up my neck and all the way to the floor. I was ready to go in a coffin, but it was okay to me. I didn't give a hoot. It was warm.

The first night I didn't sleep. I think the mattresses were stuffed with straw. It moved, and it sticked in your ass, and the noise was awful. It was not nice, I tell you. I turned and turned, and cried, and I was lost. I thought to myself, "What the hell is going to happen to me here?"

I couldn't sleep, so I just lay there real quiet and prayed.

CHAPTER TWELVE

I WISH YOU WASN'T HERE

THE FAMILY THAT OWNED THE FARM HAD COWS, CHICKENS, rabbits, and horses. When I was there farmers could have only five or six cows or something, but most times Hitler took everything away from them. The dogs jumped, jumped, jumped, jumped. They were hunting dogs and they went after rabbit, pheasant, anything that flew, and Mrs. Beckman, her boys, George and Heinrich, and the grandma talked to the dogs in German. I don't know what the hell they talked about, but the dogs listened and they followed them around everywhere.

Mrs. Beckman did the cooking. Her husband was away at war, I have no idea where, but she always dressed in black, real tall and straight, black hair all nice done. I thought she had a nice face, but it looked like she always came from a funeral; no makeup, plain, never a wrinkle. I said, "Hi, Mrs. Beckman!" No expression. She walked like a statue, and she didn't talk much, either. Most of the time she checked out the kitchen, and then she served at the bar, and she made sure the restaurant was okay.

George and Heinrich did everything with the oxen and with the skis. We had a lot of winter there, I tell you that, so everything had to be done between the few summer months, May, June, July, and August. The fog was terrible, too.

The light-haired boy, Mrs. Beckman's oldest son, Heinrich, never said a word to us. He demanded everything with the hands and with the eyes. He said, "You, you, you, you," and then we followed him with the pitchfork and pitched hay. He watched, and if we weren't working, he went over and told Eulla.

Heinrich milked the cows, he planted whatever vegetable, he called the cows in, and he could lift that hay like nobody's business. He followed exactly what Mrs. Beckman said. Every morning George went out with a big pipe and then he called, and Mrs. Beckman heard it, and understood. So Heinrich went out and piped back an answer. I loved to sit there at the table, and listen to them calling back and forth.

They loved music and yodeling. They sang, most of the time about birds. The songs were beautiful, too. But I thought Heinrich sang because he was pissed off. Heinrich was always real sad, like he missed his father. That's what I thought.

George, the dark-haired boy, was the youngest. He went up the mountains all the time on skis with a big basket on his back to get bread. Maybe he went to school somewhere in the morning, I don't know, but I only saw him working on the farm or coming down from the mountains with his skis. They had a lot of animals, so the boys took over after their father left. I don't think George liked it, but that is what happened.

George didn't care for us too much. I think the Germans moved in and took over their farm by force. Mrs. Beckman wouldn't tell us. The feeling I got from all of them was, "Don't even come near us. Just do your thing and don't bother us."

George let me know that. I was in the loft of the barn doing something with the hay. I never stacked up hay in my life, and somewhere I was not doing it right. He said in German to me, "That's not stacking!"

I said, "You can do it better?" and I threw the pitchfork down to him.

He grabbed the pitchfork and said, "Get lost!" in German. "You think I want you here?"

I said, "Well, shit," in half German and half my language, "You think I want to be here?"

So he climbed up in the loft and said, "This is what you do!"

"Good! You know how to do it? Do it!" and I took off.

George yelled to me in German, "I wish you wasn't here!"

But later George got me a beautiful Edelweiss. It's a tiny flower that looked like it was made out of yellow velvet, and in the middle is a red little thing. You have to go real high in the mountains to find it. I was so stupid, I didn't know if they were making up to me, or they wanted to kill me, or whatever.

I first met the grandma when I sneaked in the kitchen. I shouldn't have done it. I don't know the grandma's name. She was real old, gray hair, tiny, thin, with that old frailness that looked like she could crumble into powder. I didn't see an old man there, I didn't see any men, except the soldiers that came in, and so I think she was a widow. Grandma wore real stiff high-collar black dresses. It looked like one piece, like she was wrapped in a corn husk.

I looked, and there was milk standing in the kitchen, and I looked at Grandma, and I pointed at the milk. She nodded her head. So I took a little scoop, and I drank it. The milk was not cooked, by the way; it was right out of the cow, and I got the shits.

George caught his grandma letting me drink the milk one time. He was so pissed off. He said, "You shouldn't be here!" in German.

I said to him, "I had to clean the kitchen."

He said, "Yes! And my grandmother, she's not to give you anything!"

I said, "She didn't. I asked her."

During the day, Grandma walked around real slow and just watched things, and then floated back up to the house and stayed there, and then she went I don't know where. But wherever she went she was always sad. Her chin drooped all the time, and I never saw her change her face or nothing.

The restaurant was big. It opened at 9 o'clock in the morning, and it closed at 10 at night. The Germans came in and out. We were not allowed in there, so I watched through the door. You know me, I'm nosy. I had to see everything. But I thought, "Oh, that's good food." Because they had fried onions and they put a whole bunch of potatoes in, and then they set them on a big fire.

A lady named Rosie served the Germans and did the cleaning. Rosie was tiny, a little bit chubby, her hair was dark, and she wore it like the Germans did, with all the little pins in it. I have a feeling she was family, because Rosie, Mrs. Beckman, and Grandma always sat in the morning, read the newspaper, and they ate together.

Rosie drank with the Germans. You don't have a German who don't live for drink. I could see her sitting smoking with the soldiers. First they talked or something. Then they ate and drank, and then they had a box they put the records in and the German "oomp pa pa" music came on. Rosie danced and sang.

I first met her when she went upstairs to dress or whatever she did, and then we met on the stairs. She wore a beautiful white, fluffy blouse, a big skirt, and under the skirt is a big petticoat. But she did wash that with her hands. She ironed it, and she starched it, the sleeves had to stand up just so, and it was beautiful. She always said, "Hi," when we were passing. I asked her if she made her dresses, and she said she did. She spoke German well. Rosie's room was on the other side of the house. We could see the rooms, but we couldn't go there.

CHAPTER THIRTEEN

THE LULLABY IS OVER

WE BATHED ONCE A WEEK THERE, WHETHER YOU BELIEVE THAT or not. We went down to the basement where the hose was, we stood in a line, and they sprayed us off. And then they gave us a towel, and we made sure the towel was washed and hung up. They had water pumps, but the water had to be boiled before we drank it. And then there was the creek. We drank from it, and we washed ourselves in it. That water was awful cold. It was nice and healthy though.

Eulla had a whistle. My God, when she blew that whistle, you better get out of bed. If not, she started yelling. She called out role in the morning, in the afternoon, and then in the evening before we went upstairs. Every morning, we got up while it was still dark and started marching. One stone road led in and another road wound up into the mountains. Sometimes Eulla stood waiting for the girls in the morning. She would not go until everybody was in line. Most of the time we needed boots there. The other girls sent home letters, and the parents sent them boots, but I didn't have that. So most of the time I didn't go too far; I stayed close to the house and ran around the building. My feet was frozen. So I ran fast so my circulation was good, but still the snow was awful deep. It came up to my knees, you know. I got frostbite on one of my ears, too. When the weather changes and it is real cold like ice, I can feel that even now.

We marched for an hour and got breakfast afterwards. We stepped in single file and then stood there behind our chairs while Eulla talked to us and said a speech or something about Hitler. Then we said, "Heil Hitler," she said, "Sit down," and then we could sit until she tells us to eat. There was always that one table and that was it. Everything was at that table.

Eulla ate with us. But not the same food. I told you how just before lunch I sneaked in the big kitchens in the back, because there was all that good food there, they were cooking all the time, fried potatoes and vegetables that I never saw in my life, and it smelled delicious. That's not what we got. We got two slices of lousy German bread in the afternoon. We scraped the mold off before we ate it. Then we got a big slice of hard cheese. My God, I think you could lose your teeth on it. Then we had a big, huge sour cucumber. They had sauerkraut, sour red cabbage, sour this, sour that. Even the rice was sour. That's the way they cooked it, with a lot of vinegar. Then there were slimy rice balls. When I pulled them apart the slime looked like snot.

I told them, "I cannot eat that."

Eulla said, "Yes you can."

I stuck my fork in it, and the damn thing flew away and fell on the floor. She made me pick it up, clean it, and eat it. The good stuff that I liked was the red cabbage with apples. But that sour shit, I don't know why they had to put sour in there.

After that we went upstairs, dressed ourselves, and made ready for the class. There were two other teachers, Gusta and a Dutch girl from Holland.

The girls liked Gusta. She read a lot, and she wrote a lot. I didn't see her after the classes. She was in uniform. They had to be. But she was always funny.

The Dutch girl was not that old either. She did the writing in German. She always picked on me because Dutch and Belgium don't connect too good. We had to speak fluent French, and I didn't, so they knew right away I was from a different class, and then she made me clean the toilet, or do the dishes or whatever; things that lower class people did. And I hated people doing that. I couldn't stand it. I thought, "I'm going to get you for this!" And later I did.

The Dutch teacher was seeing a German officer, and I saw them going upstairs one time, and there was something going on there. I thought, "They're not going to believe me. What the hell can I do to get Eulla?" So I found a mouse in the back of the stables. I took the mouse in a box and put it in the Dutch girl's room, and the little mouse ran out. She yelled, yelled, yelled. I thought, "Oh my goodness, they're going to kill me!"

Eulla came out of her room. The Dutch girl ran out in her underwear, and the German officer followed, and Eulla saw that. Then it came out that I did the mouse. Well, she made me clean the floor. What else is new? Then they sent the Dutch girl away, and I never saw her again. It was lousy for me to do that, but I did.

We had class in the morning and work in the afternoon. What we did most was geography, map drawing, and history. When I was nice and I did something good, then Eulla said, "You watch the kids. Everyone sits like that and nobody talks or moves," and I wrote down the names of anyone that did. That was the payoff, I guess.

Eulla's hands were fantastic and nails clean. They were not big, either. She always held her thumbs and fingers together, and I thought, "Is she a preacher? Why does she hold her thumbs like that?" She had a wood and ivory stick always on the table in front of her, and we watched that thing. An old upright piano sat in that same room, and we sang all these dumb German songs while Gusta played it and Eulla waved that stick around:

Es regnet, es regnet,
Der Kuckuck ist nass
Aber wir sind trocken
Verdruss urn das

It's raining, it's raining,
The cuckoo is wet
But we are dry
Let's not bother about that

When we left the room, she always left the stick by the piano and we don't touch it either. I made jokes with Eulla to make her happy, you know, do something; pick flowers for her, or make her a card and write something on it, something like that, simple things. She looked at me, and I thought, "Uh oh." One mistake, if I said something wrong, or I read something dumb, then she said, "Stop!"

We stopped.

She said to me, "Go over that again."

I went over it again.

She said, "Stop!" Then she said to me. "Come here! Stand here. Read this again."

I read it again, made the same booboo, and then she hit my hand. She said, "Go over it again." She wouldn't say what the hell I did wrong. I went over five times the same damn thing trying to figure out what it was.

She got me books, and they were German. She said, "We have to learn German."

I opened it, and I looked. I thought, "What the hell is this for? I'm not German." So I told her that.

She came over, grabbed the book, and rolled it up. She said, "Put your hands out."

I said, "For what?"

She said, "I'm going to learn you why."

I said, "So I don't want to learn German."

She said, "Put your hands out." She hit me, "boom, boom" with the book. She said, "And never do it again."

I said, "Yavule!" And I never did, either.

Eulla made you talk German and everything else. I talked it fairly good, but I didn't keep up with it. She could control the girls. I'm telling you, they were scared from her. We sat at that big, long table, straight with our shoulders back, hands behind our backs, and she stood at the end, and we weren't to look at each other. I didn't move. I thought I was going to be crucified on the damn thing.

At three o'clock, we went outside again and ran. I don't know why. To wind us down, I guess. At night we stood by our doors, and Eulla came over and checked us out, that we did our teeth, that our ears were good, and that we didn't have nothing in our mouth from the kitchen. The lights were out by nine. We said goodnight in German, and Eulla sang Brahms' Lullaby while we stood there falling asleep. Then we went to our room, and she closed the door. The lullaby is over. I wished I would never wake up.

CHAPTER FOURTEEN

IT'S YOUR FLAG. IT'S NOT MINE

WHEN EULLA WENT OUT WITH US, THEN SHE PUT A BLACK CAP on. Eulla was healthy. She was not skinny. She had muscles. When she hit you, you lay on the floor, I tell you. One time, the camp leader came. The camp leader was like a big German asshole that inspected all the camps, an older man, tiny, like Hitler himself. They always came with two or three. We made sure the beds were clean and folded all the time perfect. He looked that the mattresses were clean and that the water was clean. When he arrived, we always raised the flag.

Gusta told me, "Rach, Eulla told me you have to raise the flag."

You know me, stupid. I said, "What would I raise the damn flag for? It's your flag. It's not mine."

She said, "Rachel. That's what Eulla said."

I said, "So what?"

She said, "You better raise that damn flag or you're going to get something."

I thought, "Why me? I'm not going to raise that dumb old flag." And I didn't. Oh God, I knew it. Eulla whistled, and she whistled, and a third time she whistled.

Gusta raised the flag.

I said, "Thank you."

Then after everything was done and the guy took off, Eulla took me to the basement. She said, "Okay, I told you," in German. "I told you to raise the flag."

I said, "Yes. But it is not my flag."

She said, "I didn't ask you. I am the boss here. Not you. I tell you to raise the flag, and you raise the flag."

I said, "No, it is not my flag."

She said, "I'm not going to tell you again. You see that hose? I put it on you."

So I told her again. My big mouth. She took that damn hose and opened it up. I flew in the corner against the wall, and it knocked me to the stone floor. Then she told me, "Go in your room and sit there, and you think about it." I cried. I thought she broke my back. I couldn't walk for two days. And after that, whatever she told me to do, I did, I tell you that.

Eulla looked at our faces and we knew right away, don't mess with her. She didn't smoke, she didn't drink. Anything with exercises she did. She said, "Jump, hang, climb." Every time I did something wrong Eulla said, "Get on the floor."

I thought, "What the hell is she going to make me do now?"

She said, "Do five pushups."

I looked at her and I said, "Why do I have to?"

She said, "Just do it. Five pushups." She watched and she always had a clock in her hand. She said, "Two more."

I said, "I can't!"

She said, "Two more."

I was skinny as hell, and I pumped and pumped.

Eulla just commanded and watched us like a hawk, believe

me. I had a feeling she was rich. They cleaned for her. I never saw her washing. Eulla did nothing. She put everything on a list. She said, "Listen, today we do this, this, this, and this. You do this, you do this, and you do this." And if we don't, we get less food. The work we did depended on the season. Sometimes we did farming. We went outside and picked all kinds of things: vegetables, chestnuts, walnuts, mushrooms, a lot of berries, Chameleon flowers, you name it. The Chamomile flowers were for tea. They're hard to pick, because they are tiny and we had to have a whole bunch. Sometimes we went to the barn and cleaned up the cow shit, and that was the worst. In the barn was a huge potbelly coal stove for the guys that worked there, to keep them warm. Other times we stayed indoors. Then we had to work on socks that went to the German soldiers in Russia. I knitted with four needles. I learned that from my grandmother.

Then we went up in the mountains and picked berries. They looked like blueberries, but they tasted better than blueberries. They gave us little baskets that had to be filled so far. Eulla wrote how much we had. I picked and picked, and every time I picked I put one in my mouth.

So I came back, and Eulla said, "How much do you have?"

I said, "Oh, I have a whole bunch." The more you picked, the more food you got, and the better the food was.

Eulla said to me, "Rachel, did you eat them?"

I said, "Nooo!! Why would I eat them?"

She said, "Shall I show you something?"

And I said, "Yeah!"

She said, "Come here. In the kitchen."

I said, "Okay." So I went in the kitchen. She said, "Look in the mirror."

And I looked at my face. My tongue was the bluest thing you ever saw.

She said, "Did you eat them or not?"

I said, "Not all of them. Once in a while I put one in my mouth."

She said, "That's better."

But anyway, the berries were fantastic.

I went to Eulla's room once. I knocked on the door to ask about studies or something. She had the best room; big, beautiful, full of books. Most were history books. She was really good at that. But never religion.

On Sunday I heard the sound of bells. A church sat up on the mountain, and I could see the dome. I loved the bell, because I was raised Catholic, I guess. I never saw a priest come in. But Mrs. Beckman always went in the morning somewhere, and I have a feeling she went to the church. I asked Eulla if I could go there. She said, "I would let you go, but you are not here for entertainment. You are in a German camp."

I was close to my uncle Michiel. He was somewhere in Germany, but I didn't know where. Eulla said, "Write him a letter." So I wrote it and she sent it away. I could not post it myself, because she had to read it first. I didn't write much. We couldn't tell each other the truth anyway, because they watched us, and they read those letters. He got the letter, because I got a letter back from him. In there he put some commas between things, so I picked that up and I read the letter over and over, and I thought, "That's funny, the commas doesn't belong there," you know. So I took all the commas and read over that, and it spelled in, "Pee in your bed."

I thought, "What does he mean pee in my bed?"

He said, "If they think you have a bladder infection, they'll bring you out to the hospital."

I thought I would try it, you know. So I did. It didn't work out like he tells me. Eulla said, "You can pee in it, you can dry it." She made me stand outside with that mattress on my head. It was really cold, and I was so pissed off at him. So I never peed again in my bed.

Aunt Amandine sent me money in the camp. They thought I could use it to buy extra food. But that was not true. The letter was opened, and the money was not there. So they took it out, I guess.

My roommate peed on her mattress. I did it on purpose, but she didn't. She got problems. She was scared because of what happened to me. So she said, "I didn't do it." She told everyone I climbed up and peed on her mattress. And that was not true. I wouldn't do that.

I cried. I thought, "What did she do that for?" She thought that was funny, but I didn't think so. But because I peed before, Eulla was not certain of me. So she checked it out. She took me to the office and closed the door. Then she said, "I want you to tell me the truth."

I was scared. I thought, "Oh God, I'm going down to the basement again." I said, "No, Eulla. I didn't. I did it the first time, yes, because I thought I was going to go to the hospital and have more food. But this time I don't. I have a feeling she is not good, and she does it."

Eulla said. "Why do you think that?"

I said, "Because in the night she is not sleeping. She always turns and turns and turns, and I can't sleep."

So Eulla said, "Okay." She said, "Don't say nothing, and I don't going to punish you."

I said, "Thank you, Eulla." And I went out.

Later on they checked her out, because she peed constantly in the bed. It was straw, so it went right through. And I was in the bottom bunk. I thought, "My God, I don't want that to happen."

I had been in camp for maybe a little over six months already. There I was not happy. I thought, "When do I go home?" Things went through my mind when I was sitting there. I was so pissed off with my mother. I thought I never was going to see her again. We never knew what was happening on the outside, and with the bombing, I thought Belgium would be gone.

CHAPTER FIFTEEN

THAT'S THE WAY PEOPLE DIE

IN THE FEW WARM WEEKS BETWEEN SUMMER AND FALL WHEN in the sky we saw some blue and some clouds and some blue and some clouds, George and Heinrich went out to the fields and cut the hay with big scythes. They could slice our legs off with those, too, if we got too close. We had to put it together and somebody came and bundled it, and then we picked it up and threw it in the wagon, and they drove it away. It was dry and the hay dust flew around. I must've been allergic to hay. I couldn't breathe.

George said, "Hurry up," in German.

I said to him, "I can't."

He said, "Why not?"

I said, "I can't breathe." My nose was running, my eyes were popping out, and I thought, "Oh God, I'm going to die here." I had the same problem with the mattress. George thought I was messing around.

Rosie always worked inside. Maybe she looked through the window or something, because she saw that I was having a problem and brought me in the kitchen to help with the milk. The milk cans are big huge things, and they're not easy. I washed them and sprayed them. But I was out of doing the hay, thank God.

In the kitchen, they had a big stove with all these heavy cast iron containers in it, and they were in there to cook. In the afternoon, Mrs. Beckman took them out. She said, "Wash the pan." So when there were some leftovers in there I, sneaky, ate them. Mrs. Beckman pretended she don't see it. They always had soup or macaroni. I loved macaroni. Then there was the fresh milk. I just scooped it up and drank it. It was not a good taste, and it was heavy and warm, because it just came out of the cow's body. But I was so hungry I ate anything.

It was early 1944. I was fourteen then. Everything we saw was propaganda. Hitler was losing like hell, but we didn't know it. I think I picked up an infection somewhere. I have a feeling that something I ate or something I drank was poison. It came on slowly, over several weeks. But I was in pain. I didn't want to lie down, because then they wouldn't give me any food. So I worked, but I had to go constantly, and then I started bleeding. When it was that bad, Eulla said, "Go to the sick room." I was really weak. Then she knew I was not joking.

They sent a letter to somebody, I don't know who it was. I don't think we had a doctor. Eulla did everything. Then she said to me, "We have to send you to a hospital." And she did all the paperwork. We knew nothing.

Gusta said, "You have to go to Brussels." She brought me back on the train. I have a feeling they called back to my mother, but she never said that. My skin turned yellow, my gums were black, and my hair fell out. I was horrible. You should've seen me. My bladder was messed up, plus my liver was gone bad, too. I think it was about two days to Brussels from the station in Wertach. They got me some pills, because I was in awful pain, so I can't remember too clearly.

When we got to Brussels, from there we took a taxi to the German headquarters in the middle of the city, a castle with German flags all over the place. The Belgium flag was out. There was one with a red circle and a swastika. You better don't touch it either. You touch one, they shoot you right there. When we passed a flag, they stopped us and said, "Didn't you salute?"

I said, "What is that?" I was so stupid.

They had to see me there first, because Germans aren't easy to believe. They checked me out and put it on the paper. Well, my stomach didn't work; I couldn't keep down the food, my bladder was infected for some reason. So they said, "Yeah."

I stayed in one of the rooms while Gusta talked to the Germans. What she said, I have no idea, but she came back and told me that I was signed off for one year, or whatever contract they made on me. But because I was sick, the contract didn't go.

I spent one night in the headquarters. When I was done there, then Gusta said, "Okay, they're going to send you to Ghent." The Germans said the best thing is not go back to my family in Ghent and don't tell nothing, just go to the hospital. When I was there in the hospital, then they would contact my mother.

From there I took the trolley bus to Ghent. It was an hour from Brussels to Ghent, and the trolley bus was not crowded. There was one soldier with me, a German, and he had a Red Cross arm patch on, but he wouldn't talk to me.

Once there, Charles, the family doctor who looked after my grandfather, picked me up. He had the car. It was an old Opal. The last thing I remembered was him laying me in the blanket in the back seat of the car and covering me up.

And then I woke up in the hospital. I was in a really white, simple room with a wash table, a bowl, and a big pitcher that the doctors washed their hands in. There were tubes in me, why I can't remember. But everything moved. I was really sick.

Charles was there wearing a white coat. He was scared for me. There were doctors and nuns. All the nurses were nuns there. There were nuns and nuns and nuns. They didn't tell me anything. They just made sure I had a nice, cozy room, and they came to me and talked to me.

First of all they checked my body out, because they didn't know exactly what I had. I was sick, my urine was not good, and I had a feeling that Eulla broke my back with the water. Maybe it was my blood. I don't know. It was real painful for me. They were scared that my kidney or something wasn't right. They did a lot of x-rays; they did a lot of inside changing. I remember swallowing tubes all the way inside my stomach. Charles had a tube on the end and took some samples, then he pulled it and the whole thing came out. He said, "Okay, now we're going to take some from here." That's the way they did it.

There is a big university behind the hospital, so students walked around there. Sometimes they'll ask you, "Can the students come in?" But that is okay, because sometimes they knew better than the doctor. The people were not a doctor there unless they had money, and not too many of the students were girls. In my time seldom did you have women who worked to be a doctor. So when the students saw me, a piece of shit born out of wedlock, they looked at me like, "You aren't worth shit."

I got so many shots. They didn't tell me what they were, but they put me to sleep. I slept a lot. Charles came and woke me up. He said to me, "Are you okay?" and he made me warm. He said, "Are you sleeping good?"

I said, "Yeah." I dreamt all the time that I was on a big mountain, and as soon as I was comfortable, I fell. I would wake up and—"No, I'm in bed." It might be my spiritual life, too. Because that was not a good picture, either. I blamed everything on the wrong person.

I was in that separate room for a week, and then I was put into the room with another lady when they found out that I didn't have a contagious disease. There were two in the room, and she lay next to me. She didn't move. Once in a while a guy came in there and looked at her, and then he touched her.

I thought she was dead. Charles said she wasn't. There were flies all over her, crawling all over her eyes, nose, and mouth. But she was still breathing.

I was going nuts. I said to Charles. "You want me to heal, you better get me away from her. Take me out, because I can't stand it." Then one morning the nun came in. She checked it, and I saw her running out, and then the doctors came, put her on the gurney, and wheeled her out. I said to the nun, "Is she dead?"

The nun said, "Yes."

I told her. "A long time she lay there like that. She don't move."

The nun said, "That's okay. That's the way people die."

CHAPTER SIXTEEN

I DO CARE ABOUT TOMORROW

I was fourteen, and I never saw my menstruation. All my cousins had theirs, and my mother was young when she got hers. The doctor said, "That's funny." So they tried to make that come normally. They put bags of heated sand on my stomach and back, and they massaged and moved my arms and legs to bring back the strength.

A young student nurse named Sister Anyes came in and sat and told me about the farm where she grew up. She described all the flowers and crops in the field, and the farm animals. She talked about her life. Most were from families who were farmers. Sometimes they went in to the convents because the parents wanted them to. The boys would be priests, the girls nuns. They paid for that, by the way. Charles said to me, "Nothing in Belgium is for free." That was not a lie, either.

She asked me about my mother and how many kids she had. Every time Geoff came over on leave my mother got pregnant, so I had no idea. They knew, but they didn't let me know anything.

Later I found out Charles didn't want my mother to come by me in the hospital. "You're here. Nobody's going to bother you." That's what he told me. He said, "And you recover."

The food they gave me was real particular. They started off with yogurt first and oatmeal and fruit. Grapes were the easiest one for me. The nurse gave me a lot of milkshakes. I don't know what was in them, but it tasted like vanilla. My stomach was not good. They were thinking that I had ulcers or something. Why, I don't know.

My nails were completely gone, my hair broke off, my gums turned black, and my teeth were loose. The doctor checked them. My teeth were good, but my gums were rejecting them. So they put something on them, like a glue. It was a horrible taste, I tell you that. They came in with my medicine and Charles told me not to talk. For my hair they took a brush and inside was electricity. Charles went over my scalp. It's funny but it's true. I really didn't feel it, but I thought they were going to fry my brain.

Once in a while the nun came in and had a conversation. Got me back to the Lord, I guess. But I was really cautious about that. I still remembered my confirmation. Sister Anyes just said, "Well, it's a man, and you know a man. You should forgive him."

I told her, "He should've given the Missal to me. I don't care what I was, a whore, a bastard, or whatever. I should've gotten it."

She said, "Yes, see, you remember."

I said, "I don't want to remember."

Sometimes Charles came in and brought books and made me read. Most of them were doctor's books; you know, about bodies and stuff, or books with different stories. I couldn't read very well, either. He told me that was the best way to get my education. He sat and we talked and he listened. He always looked at my face, smirking, and I told him, "Why are you always looking at me?"

He said, "Because I want to see your reaction."

I hated that. I thought I did funny stuff.

The nuns came by me, and they helped me with reading and arithmetic. They prayed with me and they talked about Jesus, and I told them, "No, I don't want to hear about Him." I was not ready. But they did it anyway.

After about a month I was finally able to get up out of bed to use the toilet or bathe or sit in a chair while the nuns changed my bed.

The hospital was in two sections. One was connected to the church and the priests, one went to the hospital and all the rooms. In the rooms was two beds, two beds, two beds. Everybody that died in the hospital went to the chapel and the priest took care of the funeral. When they had money, they took them out in another funeral in a bigger church. The outside was a big beautiful lawn with a fountain in the middle. Most of the time the nuns picked me up in the lobby and took me wherever I had to go.

Sister Anyes told me about the choir of nuns that sang for the services in the hospital. She wanted to take me to the early mass when I got stronger. The church services were early morning, because the nuns had to go right to work in the hospital, so the nuns helped me to walk to the services. I was in my hospital gown, with a coat on over it. They had special coats.

The services were long. First of all the nuns sang. They sang like angels. After all this, then the priest went up and read off who died, who was born, who was going to live, and who was going to die, and a whole bunch of nonsense to me.

The churches were always big there. Everybody paid for their lousy chairs. Now I don't think they do that anymore, but then I sat down and he said to me, "You have to pay a quarter." Back then a quarter was a lot. I didn't have a quarter, so I was standing. He said, "Well, you cannot stand either."

I said, "Well, I'm not going to stand," and I just left.

Around that time, somebody in the neighborhood that knew me told me to go over and see my grandmother. Something happened to her, so somebody brought me from the hospital to her, but I don't know who it was now.

My grandmother was living in a little apartment in the city at that time. She got a nice pension from my grandfather, so when Fredric and Marie were settled and they were comfortable in my grandmother's old house, they found a little apartment in the city and they put her in there with some little furniture and a little bed, they took the money, and they took care of her, paying the bills and clothes.

When I came in, my grandmother was lying on the bed. Then I talked to her and she said she fell down, or something like that. The house was a mess, so before I left to go back to the hospital I tried to clean it up for her as fast as I could. My aunt Sofie was living there with my grandmother at the time, and as I was straightening up the house, the door flew open and Sofie ran in with an ax and started axing the house. I was stunned. I didn't know what to do, and my grandmother was paralyzed. It was a small place, so she smashed everything.

The apartment was on a little corner, and the neighbors heard the noise. Nobody had a phone then, so some girl across the street ran to a police department on the corner, and they called somebody who came out with a wagon and bound Sofie up in a straightjacket. They got a white sheet over her and loaded her into the car in a gurney.

I had to go back to the hospital, so the neighbor said to me, "I'll take care of your grandma. You go back." I didn't know why Sofie did that, because she raised me. Later I was told Sofie's husband Lionel came back to Belgium. He was in Germany for some reason. She knew he was coming and went to the train station to meet him. He got off the train with a woman. He said to her, "I have some news for you." So she was happy. Then he said,

"This is my new wife."

Sofie said, "Huh?" Then she started hitting him and hitting him. That's when she ran home. She could run.

I made it to my fifteenth birthday in the hospital. I think it was the summer. I'm not certain, though, because I never celebrated any of my birthdays. Charles was pretty close to his patients. He was always alert and looked at his watch. "Oh, I have to go look at that patient." He didn't have too much else, but people loved him. Nobody from my family came to see me in the hospital, so sometimes he brought me flowers or something.

In my mind I was in a real war situation. At that moment I hated the whole world I think; my mother, my stepfather, my grandmother, I didn't want to see nobody. I didn't believe no more that God was there to help me. I thought He dropped me somewhere. Charles said to me, "Don't say that. That's not true."

My hair and nails were taking a long time to grow back. My nails never came in normal. They peeled and every time I touched them they broke off. I started biting them all the time. Charles was pissed off. He said, "I have to do something with that." So he let somebody come and do my hair and my nails, and I looked so good. He said to me, "You like that, huh?"

I said, "Yes."

He said, "Good. You bite one more nail, and you're going to see something."

So he coated them with something. I don't know what the hell it was, but, boy, was that a taste. I never bit them again. My hair came out, my nails began to grow, and my weight came back. I walked in the hospital gardens with the nun to breathe the fresh air and to see the flowers. At first I couldn't see beauty in nothing.

I thought a lot. The future was always scary for me.

Charles told me. "Don't worry about tomorrow. Today is what we worry about." He always told me that.

I said, "I do care about tomorrow." I told him, "I don't want to go back to my mother. So what? Then I go through the same shit again. What if I didn't have you? What would happen to me?"

He said, "Well, there's always somebody. They're going to pick you up. The Red Cross or somebody. You will find out later on, things are going to get better."

I said, "When?" I asked him, "Is it not better just to let me die?"

"No." He said, "You have to change your attitude."

CHAPTER SEVENTEEN

IF YOU EVER TALK ABOUT THIS, THAT'S IT FOR YOU

ONE DAY CHARLES BROUGHT ME CLOTHES, AND HE PUT A HAT on my head because I didn't have any hair, and he took me out all the way to the ocean. I never saw it look so beautiful. We were sitting and he said, "Now you see the ocean. Now that we're outside, you can talk."

I had a cup of coffee and a little pastry, really nice and cozy. He said, "Now, I'm going to show you how you eat pastry and drink coffee."

I said to him, "Don't you think I can drink a damn cup of coffee?"

He said, "Yes, but not the way that you learned it. I will teach you how." He said, "You hold the saucer in your lap with your left hand, stir the coffee like so, place the spoon on the right side of the saucer, raise the cup in your right hand, sip it, place it back on the saucer."

I said to him, "You have to be kidding me."

"Yes, you do. I want you to learn to go back to society, because you didn't learn proper etiquette at all," he said.

Slowly he brought me back to the world. I don't know what he did, but I thought, you know, I'm going to kill him when it's over. He brought me back to the hospital afterwards, and then I went back to my bed. He said, "And don't talk."

"Okay," I said.

Never inside; always by the mountains, or the roses, or the ocean. "That's love," he said, "and that is the air, and that is God's creation."

I thought. "Hmm." Then I was pissed off. I felt I was like a kitchen sink full of scum that had to be cleaned.

He said, "No, that's nothing to do with it. I want you go back into society, and you look like a lady." He said, "You don't see yourself. I see you. I will teach you."

We went to dinner one time. I said to him, "How the hell do rich people eat that's so different?"

He said, "Listen, all your life all that you had was one little this, a scoop of potatoes, mustard in the middle, and stir it up and eat it." He said, "No. There is more to life than potatoes like you eat." So he laid out the salad, then the soup (I already knew about that) and then steak (I already knew about that) and vegetables, and whatever, and he said, "Okay. Don't stir it now. I'll show you how." Then again, a big fight. Every lousy thing we ate. But that's the way he taught me. I was so stupid.

When he bought clothes for me, he said. "You come out beautiful."

I said. "I don't like it."

He said, "You look perfect." And we fight and fight.

Charles talked to the priest at the hospital, and then I met him in his office with Charles. The priest's sister came over, and then he asked her if it was okay that I worked with her in the kitchen, and helped her out, and she said, "Yes." I think she was looking for somebody like that.

Charles said to me, "You know what? You can go there, and then you can come in the hospital any time you need to, for therapy or whatever." They didn't pay me, but Charles wanted it that way. He said, "I want you to go in there just to revive." He knew I was really upset about my mother and my stepfather, too, and he wanted me to have something to do other than to think about that.

They called the priest "Holy Father." He was in his forties, fifties. He had a beautiful face, blue eyes, with cheeks rosy like apples. He was real light blond and looked gray. In Belgium, sometimes they're gray before their time. He was like that. He had a special voice. That is for sure. When he opened his mouth, everybody obeyed. Except me.

Education had to be tough or he wouldn't be a priest. He had the two languages, and Latin. He wore black, a white collar, black shoes, except when he was working he had a little shirt on. He went in the emergency when somebody died, and as soon as the phone rang, he left. He was serious for certain reasons, but he could be happy. Most of the time when his dinner was over, I brought him his coffee and so on, and he said, "Thank you for this."

I called the priest's sister "Madam." I don't think she was married. She took care of her brother, I guess. She dressed simple, decent, in mostly dark colors, black, brown, and gray, always a coat and a hat and gloves. She didn't smile too much. I heard her typing all the time, so I think she did some writing. Maybe the mass for the priests. I think she was a little bit older than her brother, and she did his paper work and the money, and came with me in the kitchen and taught me. Remember I was fifteen. I knew a coffee pot, and I knew the toast, but I couldn't cook. So I learned a lot from her.

She got me the black uniform with the white collar. When somebody came by, I had to open the dumb door, too. Except the nuns. The nuns came in the back. I never had to open the door for them.

The three of us went to church in the morning, and when we came back, he stayed behind, and we set the table, and made the waffles, pancakes, toast, or whatever we got for breakfast. Most of the time we had sweet bagels.

I mopped the floors in the evening and cleaned the kitchen. I went from room to room dusting the furniture. Mostly it is rugs there, so it is easy to clean. The priest's sister took care of the bedrooms. I never saw their bedrooms, never. The rooms are pretty little in Europe. They're not big like here. It had only one bed, a chair, a little dresser, and a window. They had a little reading room, you know, where all the books are, two chairs, the fireplace, and they sit there. They never sat in the front in the salon.

An old Italian girl came in and helped me out in the kitchen when they had a big meal, like for Easter or a holiday. I could make the little dishes, you know, but a big dinner, when a family came over or friends, then the cooking lady came and I served the table. But they had to pay her. She was a Catholic, by the way. Nobody went in there but a Catholic. She liked to cook pastas, and I didn't know anything about that. She made perfect soups. Me, I dumped everything into the soup. Not there. It had to be nice and creamy. But anyway, she was a good cook. Most of the time the priest and his sister drove out to a big villa outside of town where another priest lived, and he drove with me in the back. Then I sat in the kitchen and did the dishes.

I still had treatments in the hospital on my stomach. I didn't go out, except with Charles. He came by and picked me up after six, and then we drove. He got his practice going pretty good, and he was known there. His cousin was the chief of the hospital. They got meetings there, the students came to him, and so he was pretty busy. If it was urgent, he let me come through, but most of the time we met somewhere else.

I don't know if I should tell you this. I was crazy about Sister Anyes. So I always hung on her for attention. The bell of the back door rang. I opened the door. There was Sister Anyes. Then she said, "I have a meeting with the Holy Father."

I said, "Okay." So I let her in. I went back to the kitchen, and a little while later she left. When she left, I saw drops of blood on the floor. I thought, "What the hell is she bleeding for?" I was young. I never got my menstruation like a normal girl. I always saw the nuns coming in, and after Sister Anyes left blood spots on the floor, I thought, "What happened? Why was she bleeding?" I thought she had a sore or something. But I was so stupid, too. Every afternoon the nuns came in, always it was a different nun, beautiful looking. I thought, "I have to know what the hell they are doing!"

They had a big, huge keyhole; you know the old fashioned ones? So I looked through it, and I could see her habit hanging on the chair. I thought, "Why did she take that off?" So I went to the other office and looked through that keyhole, and then I knew what the priest was doing with her. And I thought, "Oh my God!" You know what I mean?

So then I called Charles. I said, "Charles, I have to talk to you!"

He said, "What now?"

I said, "Just get me out somewhere! I want to talk to you alone!" He picked me up in the evening, and we went somewhere he knew, and I told him the story.

He said, "You know what?" He took a piece of bread and he stuck it in my mouth and said, "Don't you ever, ever say anything about that! If you ever talk about this, that's it for you."

My eyes were like saucers, and I said to him, "They are married with God!"

He said, "Yeah, but the priest has to take care of them."

And I thought, "My God!" But that's the truth. So I said, "Well, that's it. I'll never go to church again!"

He said, "But you have to. He is there in the morning and you have to go with him."

"Okay, but I'm not going in that damn confession booth with him again." I said, "And I don't want to stay there when it is that bad."

"Okay," he said. "Then we look for something else. In the meantime, you're still connected with the hospital. You are not healthy yet, and nobody's going to pay for you. So just keep your mouth zipped and leave the nuns alone." He said, "Later in your life you will realize what is said and what is not."

I didn't like that priest anymore, and Anyes, I don't know. I hated that. I stopped completely going to church.

CHAPTER EIGHTEEN

THAT'S NOT THE END. THE WORST IS YET TO COME

CHARLES NEVER WANTED ME TO GO BACK TO MY MOTHER, because he knew my family. But I wanted to go because I loved her all the time. I didn't like what she did, but I was close to her.

In the war they bombed different people that we knew. Either that or they left in the war, or they were shot, or they were widowed. So a lot of changing in the war came.

Some things stayed the same. My family still lived on the same street. Edmond, the middle brother, still had his house. Fredric, the eldest brother and his wife Marie, lived in my grandmother's house. Fredric was with the Whites, the Resistance from Belgium. Marie got a baby in the war. Michiel's wife, my aunt Amandine had another boy they named Fredric. Amandine came from Germany to stay with her mother. They made good money in Germany, but she didn't go back, because of the boy. So my uncle Michiel later came along back to Belgium. Then Jenny lived next to them. Jenny's husband Erwin was a watchman working for the Nazis, but not by choice. We didn't know where Erwin was. He was in Mariakerke there, but he was not home either. My mother was still living with Jenny and her daughter Stéphanie.

My sister Sarah, the surviving twin, was now four years old, and my brother Antoine was two. He looked like my mother. My sister and my brother, they all had blue eyes. I didn't.

My mother was pissed off. She said to me, "I'm going to have a bad name because of you." She thought it was my fault that the Germans sent me back, that they couldn't control me. She said. "The Germans are going to say you never made that year, you can't discipline yourself, this and this." We didn't have good communication. Forget it. But she was my mother.

I didn't see my grandmother much anymore. She was happy to see me when I came back. After what my grandfather said, I knew I was going to go through trouble. But when I got back my grandmother said, "That's not the end. The worst is yet to come, because now the Americans will come in and your mother is going to start having problems."

I didn't see much of the kids after I came back, because they were in the playpen, and they stayed in there, and I was back and forth working. I got work wherever I could. Sometimes my neighbor Stella said, "Rachel, can you clean my house?"

I also got a job at the cotton mill again. The Congo was closed, so the mill no longer used cotton, but now made carpets of floss. It was a big factory with rows and rows of long machines. We had a heavy sack hanging around our waist. There were two other girls on the same machine. At the weavery we had ten hours work, and they didn't pay that good. But whatever I could get to make more money, I jumped on it.

Once in a while Geoff jumped over on leave. The last time I saw Geoff before the war ended he came for a short time to make another kid, I guess. Every time I said to my mother, "I'm not taking care of it!"

She said, "Yes! You take care of it." So I did.

I stayed away from Geoff when he was in uniform. Every time he came back my mother moved again. This time they moved from Mariakerke into another house in Ghent.

I was visiting on my two days off. It was night, and we walked to their new house in Ghent. There is a castle and a gate all the way to the railroad. As we were passing by, I bumped into a warm body in the dark leaning next to the gates of the castle. But I felt clothes, you know. I had the kids in the wagon, and Geoff was messing around with my mother. I had a feeling that maybe it was a Jew or somebody who was running away from the Germans. It was always dark at night. When they caught you, they killed you. Maybe he wanted us to just go away because he don't want us to see him. That's what I thought, but I never heard anything more about it.

Later when we went home, past the ships lying there, we had to walk along a siding before we came to the house. Remember all the boats on the water? One houseboat was for years there, and we always went there for onions. I heard somebody yelling, "Help! Help!" I thought to myself, "What happened?" I told Geoff and my mother, and Geoff put a finger to his lips, so we left. I knew in my mind there was somebody drowning.

In the morning, the lady who lived in the houseboat, her father fell between the boat and the wall, and he drowned. I always thought about that. I would've gone and knocked on the door. I could've saved him. But Geoff told me I couldn't.

After that, Geoff left again, and my mother couldn't afford to pay rent on that house, so she went back to Jenny.

There was a big company where people worked that the Germans took over, and they had watchmen that walked around it. My cousin Florence passed by there all the time, and she fell in love with a watchman in the black uniform. He was on the German side. She was all the way gone for him. She said to me, "I want to see Maurice. Can you help me?"

I said, "Is it that important?"

She said, "Yeah! I want to see him!"

So me, again, I always fall into things. One day, I was standing there keeping a lookout, and they were in the little guard house kissing up a storm, and there comes her father on the bicycle. I thought, "Oh shit! What now?" I didn't know what to do, so I turned around and I pretended I didn't see him. But Fredric knew I saw him, and I knew he was going to come over and hit me. I turned around, and I said, "Florence, your father's coming!"

She said, "What now!"

Maurice said, "Stand behind me, and I'll hide you," and he told me, "You go forward and get him talking to you."

So Florence stood behind the guy. He had a big coat with his gun, and she hid under that coat so far as she could, so Fredric couldn't see her.

So there came my uncle, and he saw me standing with the German watchman. Flapped me around, "poom, poom, poom," "Go home!"

I said, "Okay! Okay!" Then he rode off. There was a little street, so I went in the street, and I waited until Florence came out, and then we went home together. She tiptoed in the house like a puppet, she went upstairs and didn't say nothing, and I came in, "boom, boom, boom," and Fredric said, "What were you doing with the German watchman!" And he grabbed me again, and I got it again from him.

The watchman broke up with Florence. He called me and he said, "Get out, whatever you do. Because I don't want you mixed up with this." So she did. But she cried a river.

I do remember when the war ended. I was home visiting. In the beginning there was some shooting going on, not much. It didn't take long. France, they helped the Americans. They were really nice, the French. The Americans were closing in.

My mother didn't know that. We didn't have TVs then or radio, so we didn't know who the hell they were. We heard it on the street from people. I was working somewhere I think. They said, "Hey, go home because something is going to happen today." And they didn't tell you what, but they warned you to stay away from the street.

Across the canal from Jenny's house were a row of big villas. The canal is only a few feet from her house, and the canal is maybe twenty-four feet wide. Then there was a small street, the row of houses with tiny fenced-in backyards, and behind them there were big open fields. The Germans were across the canal in the villas, and in the back of us in the fields were other soldiers, I don't know who. I think it was the Whites. They were shooting over the houses at each other. The bedrooms were upstairs, and we knew we couldn't go up there. My mother told me, "They're shooting. Come to the basement."

Nosy, I wanted to know what was going on. So, stupid me, I sneaked up the stairs and went to the window. I saw a German guy up in a tree, and I thought, "What the hell is he doing in the tree?" He saw me and shot right through the wall. It went "Zzziip! Poof!" I went fast down, because I thought it was in my ear. Lucky for me, he didn't hit me. My mother screamed at me, "Come down! Come down!" She said, "I'm going to kill you!"

And I said, "Well, who cares?"

We had the last house on the street, and Fredric's house was just over the wall. I had a feeling that any minute the Germans would come in shooting, or they would drive a tank through the house, because the Germans were in the front shooting, the Americans were in the back shooting. I thought, "Oh my goodness." I just wanted to get out of that house. Fredric called me to see if I was home safe. So I started crawling over the wall to Fredric's house. But Fredric screamed, "Get Down!! Get Down!!"

I slid down again and went back and told my mother, "I could not go to the front, and I couldn't go through the back." Then I cried. Because I was stuck in the house.

The Americans came around the back fields and seized a castle on the corner on the far end of the row of houses next to Edmond's house. The water was between the Americans and the Germans, but there was the railroad crossing over the canal. We have to walk real slowly so we don't fall through the ties. But the Americans were smart. They put some things between the ties, and they crawled. There was a little ferry boat that we could pay to bring us over the canal and it was attached to a wire that went from one side to the other. The Americans used that to get across the water. As soon as the Americans were close to them, the Germans threw the damn guns away, and then we saw them walking with their hands up. They were happy to see the Americans. I think some of the Germans were so relieved it was finally over they didn't want to lift a finger no more. "Take me, I'm going to get food," you know.

The Americans worked hard. They really did a good fight. My God, I was so thankful to the Americans, because they fought those damn Germans and they won, too. Germany was strong sons of a guns, and smart, too. When Hitler lost against Russia, then he crumbled all the way.

The Belgium people were happy to see the Americans, believe me. You should've heard the people, screaming, and music, and whatever. The American officers paraded with jeeps. The Americans were pretty, dressed in brown and green, and they were clean. Some of them had helmets on; some of them had beautiful caps. They were all happy people, and I was happy.

Everybody was waving and I stood, and I waved too. My mother just hit me again, you know. She said to me, "Shut up, because they are not that good, and they are a bunch of—" Well, think about it. To us, Americans were millionaires. They were giving food out of trucks. Packages with eggs, packages of milk. It was all dry stuff, dehydrated. We didn't have shit, you know. My mother took it and threw it away. I have nothing lousy to say about the Americans. They were to me gentlemen first-class. I didn't complain about them, never. They were compassionate, because we were hungry, and they knew it. Sometimes they gave us chocolate. The first chocolate I tasted I thought I would drop dead.

After the Americans came in, then the Resistance was safe and came out right away like ants. Most of the time they were men. The Resistance painted swastikas on all the doors of people they knew had been on Hitler's side. They picked up a lot of the girls that were messing around with the German soldiers there. They didn't like that either. They knew every one of them. Believe me, they did. They shaved their heads, painted black swastikas on their heads, and brought them in big wagons, and they drove them all over real slow, and everybody threw eggs at them. I was sick to have seen that. Men they took to jail, and a lot of people were hanging up, too. The big shots. But I didn't go and watch that. They hanged both men and women who were working in the big office for the Germans. The Americans didn't interfere.

About two or three days after that, the Resistance came to the house early in the morning. They were already at work during those days. I was there in the house in the kitchen, feeding the kids maybe when they came in. They were in the white khaki Belgium uniforms. They asked, "Where's Helene Van Meers?"

My mother came and said, "Here I am," and they took her outside. I thought "What the hell happened? Are they going to shoot her?"

Jenny said, "Don't talk! Don't talk!"

But I said, "To hell with you!" My sister and brother were in the chairs sleeping, so I ran out to my mother. I saw this swastika on the door, and the commissaris got my mother. They stood her against the wall with her hands up. They didn't hold her, but she couldn't move either, or they would've shot her. The neighbors all stood outside watching. They all knew she sent me to a German camp. The family did, too, but the family most of the time didn't say anything. I think it was more my neighbors that were hating my mother for what she did to me.

Fredric didn't come out. I don't know if he was home, but I think he was. Most of the time when something was up he would come over and help me. This time he didn't, so I knew it was something to do with him.

They wanted to burn the furniture. Everybody that was working with the Germans, their furniture was moved outside. Some neighbors that didn't like my mother were calling her names, "Coward," and "Traitor." My mother laughed. She was crazy, I don't know. They said, "And you don't laugh, coward, and don't do this to your daughter, coward!"

I looked, and I thought, "Uh oh. They're going to kill her for me." I went to her, and I said, "Don't you touch my mother!"

My neighbor Stella came from next door, and she hugged me, and she said, "Nothing is going to happen to you, Kleine. I make sure of that." Then the police took my mother away for interrogation, and I screamed and screamed. I thought I was never going to see her again. I didn't know what they were going to do. I told the policeman, "I can't do anything! I have the kids! I have the kids!"

The Whites said, "Just go inside and nothing is going to happen to you."

Stella had red hair. Stella's husband was in a German camp. She was alone there, and she thought he died. None of them knew if their husbands were going to come back, and he came back, lucky for her. She was one of the neighbors that was screaming the names at my mother. So she took me into her house, and I went in and screamed and cried, you know. I never trusted someone with red hair.

An hour or two later, my mother came walking back. They cut her hair off, you know.

I said to her, "What happened?"

"Well," she said. "I have to go to court." And she told me. That was the first time I knew that she signed the papers for Geoff to send me to the camp.

Meanwhile, Geoff was out hiding. They found him by a farm somewhere. He saw the state troopers coming on bicycles. Geoff thought, "Uh oh, they're going to get me." He had a hand grenade, so he threw it. They picked it up and threw it back, and then it blew up. Something happened to his eyes, dust or whatever, and he couldn't see too good. So they took him in the prison. In the prison there was a German doctor who healed his eyes. So he can be thankful for that. But after he came out, he always wore really thick glasses. That didn't change his attitude. He was still a lousy stinker, you know. But anyway, that is what happened to him, so far as I know from the stories. I never thought I would see Geoff again.

CHAPTER NINETEEN

YOU HAVE TO LIVE WITH IT

AFTER THE WAR IT WAS A MESS. FIRST OF ALL WE LOST THE KING that we liked, Leopold III. I don't remember exactly what happened, but Hitler took the whole royal family away. A lot of people thought Leopold should've never listened to Hitler, and they resented that he surrendered Belgium. So when Leopold came back from Germany they didn't like him no more.

His brother Charles took over for a little while till Leopold's son Baudouin was ready. Charles was never king, but he stepped in as Regent in 1944. Charles was always somewhere in Belgium incognito drinking up a storm with a lot of friends. Once in awhile he came there to Ghent, too, to the wrestling matches. When you saw him he was always in normal clothes and looked like a slob, that you thought he was a normal guy, but he was the prince.

After Leopold left, then the Congo wanted to be separated from Belgium, and they said, "We don't need you no more." So in 1960, the new king, Baudouin, he was a real nice person and everything, he said, "Okay, you want to be free? Well, sign the papers then. You're free." Once the Congo was gone, the cotton no more came in to Belgium. But then other things came in so the king didn't care. After that the Congo always had problems and problems and problems. There was a revolution there, nuns were killed, and raped, and you name it. But the king said, "That's it. You wanted it for your own. Don't ask us for help." And America has to take care of it.

The war did change a lot of the people. Some of them was harder. They were not that humbled like you think. When the people found out what went on during the war in the concentration camps, a dark feeling of gloom swept over all of Europe, and the religions went out. A lot of people lost their faith. The church was not like it used to be. It had nothing to do with weddings no more, and the people rejected it more, and became looser.

At that time the pope, Pius XI, was with Germany and he signed agreements with Hitler, and I think that did a lot of damage to the church in Europe. The people resented that really bad. Lucky for him he died. So then the guy from Poland came in, and he saved a lot of people. So some went back to the church, but still it was no more like it used to be.

There were a lot of missing people. They disappeared; we didn't know where they were. Some of them came back, but I don't know how many. I do know the diamond factory came back, and the beautiful restaurants came back. Not right away after the war, but still they came back, so where they were and where they went, I have no idea. But I bet they were somewhere in Sweden or in America until the war was over.

During the war everything was bombed and bombed and bombed. It was a disaster there, you know. In Ghent it was not as bad, but they still bombed all the bridges out, and the roads, and the railroads, so we were stuck wherever we were. We could not walk over the bridges; we could only cross over in a little boat, and we had to live with it.

Belgium was in ruin for awhile. I don't think nobody at that moment knew what to do, because the king had to go, and this had to change, and that had to change. Most people they were staying in wrecks, or in somebody's apartment, or in somebody's room. My mother lived in a house where the owner rented the rooms out. Because they knew there was no housing, they got away with it. We had to use the same kitchen, remember that, so I could use the kitchen maybe from 11–12 o'clock, and that's the way we lived. Whatever money they could take away from us, they did. I didn't like it, but that's what happened.

And then slowly they started cleaning up and rebuilding, and the rebuilding was better, because anything that they did was bigger and better in material. They came and tore out the lousy railroad and put in a beautiful railroad. And the houses, too. They took out all the block houses, and they put in beautiful apartments. And the roads were better.

We had coal during the war, so when we didn't have coal, we didn't have heat. But after the war they went over to gas and electric. When they rebuilt it, I think things were much better for them. More people had radios. There was a lot of business from America that they picked up, too. That was better, because Ford had his company there, so cars came in, stoves came in, iceboxes came in, but not that big like we have now. Before the war, we didn't have iceboxes, and certainly not an electric stove. They brought ceiling fans in, too, with beautiful crystal and stuff. Before we didn't have that.

The food did improve, but even after that we still ate potatoes. That is a big thing there, and vegetables, and meat or fish, one of the two. But we had more food, and big supermarkets came in. The Belgium people loved that, so the little stores lost out to the supermarkets. Everything is big now, like here in America. They have big cars there, but the streets are still small, so it's horrible.

Most houses still don't have a garage, because they didn't think about that.

Right after the war, there were a lot of homeless people. The Salvation Army, they took care of them. They had big buildings where they put them in, you know. Salvation Army did a lot of good things there. Don't let me talk about the Red Cross. But the Salvation Army was beautiful people. I liked them.

Everybody in Belgium made it better than before. My family made it better off, that I do know. They started working more, because of the rent, more employment and more kids. They made retirement shorter there, at age fifty, so there was room for other people. There was a big shuffle to have more education, and improved learning, and they got better jobs, too.

After the war we saw a lot of people who lived together, but they were not married. Most people don't want to get married yet, so they lived together first, then they get married later. Well, the Catholics didn't agree with it, you know, but the people said, "Hey, I do what I want," because they really didn't believe like American people did.

Before the woman stayed home and they got babies after babies after babies, and the man worked. So she was more hungry, and the kids were hungry. After the war that changed, too. She said, "Hey, forget that. We don't want to go like the parents, so no more kids." So the doctors gave her something that she don't have kids no more and they both worked.

So a lot of things changed, politics, attitudes, everything, and I don't think it was all for the best. But who knows, you know? I didn't like it, but I didn't stay that long there after that.

CHAPTER TWENTY

I NEED THOSE STOCKINGS

WHEN THE RESISTANCE TOOK MY MOTHER, AT THE SAME TIME they took Edmond and Aunt Sarah's furniture. Don't ask me why, but that's what happened. My aunt Sarah went by her sister next door and cried. Sarah's sister was married to a guy who owned a big coal company. Right away they called some big shot somewhere, and they said, "Uhn uh. You're not doing that. That is my sister, and you bring all those things back. Whatever you want, you pay for it." So in the morning, Edmond paid to get it out of storage. But, in the meantime, her house was empty.

Remember, Charles was the family doctor, so he knew everything. Charles asked my aunt Jenny about my mother, and my aunt said, "Well, that and that happened." I had to go into court with her. Charles told me, "Don't say nothing, just listen to what they say." He said, "I'm going to be in the courtroom, but don't let anybody know that I'm there."

So in the morning I went to the court building in Ghent, up lots of marble steps, and through a big hallway with all the doors.

There was hundreds of people there. It was a real emotional situation after the Germans were gone.

So I went in there alone and I sat and waited until the judge came in. He was an older man in a black robe with long sleeves and a white collar. After that, my mother was brought in with five or six other people. They were there for the same thing, working with the Germans. I only cared about my mother. The rest, I didn't know what they did.

Someone read off a name, and then said, "Stand up!" They told what they did, the judge slammed the gavel "Boom!" "So much," and then the next one stood up, his name, "Boom!" "So much."

I was scared. My mother was next in line. I stood up, and the judge asked me what they did in the camp, so I said, "Well, it was for discipline, and I came out because I was sick. I don't know what it was, but I had a kidney infection, and I didn't go back no more."

The judge slammed the hammer and said to my mother, "Two years in jail."

I said, "Well, I'm sorry, but she has two kids. I'm too small to take care of them."

The judge said, "Yes, but your mother has to pay for this."

I said, "Well, she should be free. She went through it, she paid for it, and now she has two kids she has to take care of. I don't know what to do. I have to work because none of them have an income here."

So the judge said, "Okay. We'll talk about it later then." So my mother had to sit down. After the other people were over, the judge asked if they had anything to say about it, and none of them stood up. They all kept their mouths shut. They thought, "Well, I better not tell him anything because maybe he slams us more years."

After it was over, I went out and walked, and then Charles drove after me and waved for me to get in. I jumped in the car, we drove off, and then he told me, "Listen, I'm going to find a lawyer and get her out of there." So he did, and they settled out of court. I don't know what happened, but one day later my mother came out.

After I quit with the priest I didn't have a place to live. Charles said to me, "Go back to your mother and stay with her, because they can't find Geoff, she's alone and she needs you." My family never knew that Charles and I were that close, and I never talked about it.

I said, "Okay." So I moved back in to my Aunt Jenny's house with my mother and my brother and sister.

One day, Jenny went shopping with Stéphanie. She had to cross the street, an American jeep passed her, but they didn't see Stéphanie and hit her. The American guy had to be a big shot, because he did everything. Stéphanie had a concussion or something, and they took her right away to the hospital in the jeep, and they took care of her. She was okay. The Americans brought her food, and when she got out of the hospital, they came over and checked her out.

The American troops were there for a month in 1944. The last night the Americans were there, the Canadians and English were still there, they had a dance in a big ballroom in the evening. I was young then. My cousin Nathalie said, "They are going to give out stockings!" We didn't have stockings, and I wanted stockings. So Nathalie said, "You can't come, because you have to baby-sit the kids."

I thought, "No! I'm going to go and get the damn stockings."

Nathalie said, "She's going to beat the hell out of you."

I said, "Well, I don't care. I need the stockings."

Nathalie said, "You got to be kidding. You're not going to do that are you?"

I said, "Oh yeah."

My mother slept with Jenny. She slept real fast, so when I heard their snoring I thought, "That's it." I crawled over the wall, went "poom!" on the ground, and I went to that big ball. It was a big café with a dance floor, and a juke box. I don't think I looked too good. I looked like Cinderella with the blouse and stupid skirt, and lousy, crooked shoes. Everything I had was second hand from my cousins. But I didn't give a shit.

When I got there they were asking for dance people. I said, "I want to dance." My aunt Sarah's brother, Bené de Loof, was there. He was a wrestler; eleven times he was a champion from Belgium. I said, "Bené! I want to get in!"

He said, "What do you want to do here?"

I said, "I want their stockings!"

He said to me, "You cannot go in. They are all Americans, and they are all big people. You are too young for that."

I said, "I don't give a shit. I want those stockings."

He said, "Okay. I close my eyes, and I didn't see you."

The dance hall was all decorated in silver streamers, and tables and all the old fashioned stuff. A band of soldiers were playing big band American jazz, waltzes, and chop chop chop, the whole saboo, you know. They would trade off and people would dance. The Belgium people are still like that; they love to dance.

A guy said to me, "I'm going to dance with you!"

I said, "I can't dance."

He said, "Don't worry about it. Just follow me."

They were American dances, the jitterbugs, and the tango, and whatever it was. I didn't even know what I was doing. I just followed the guy, and we went through everything. I flew across the floor, and I came back. Remember, I was tiny. I flew like a feather all over the place, and I won the stockings!

The day after the newspaper came out and guess what? I was on the front page dancing with the Americans. My mother, oh my God. She got her laundry stick, I went under the bed, out of the bed, and she chased me. She hit me with that stick: "Poom!

Poom! Poom!" I got bruises all over my body. I said, "Bullshit! I wanted the stockings. I don't give shit about the Americans!" My mother grabbed the damn stockings and threw them in the fire, and I cried. I said to her, "I'll hate you as long as I live!" I shouldn't have said that but I did.

So later Nathalie said, "I saw the newspapers. Where are the stockings?"

I said, "Ask my mother."

Fredric came over and saw my bruises. Boy, was he pissed at my mother. My mother said, "She sneaked out and danced at the Americans' party!"

"That don't give you the right to beat her like that," he told her. "Your job is to take care of your kids. Don't ever touch her again!"

But then he beat me himself.

We had a neighbor named Denise. They bombed the block house where she lived. They called it a block house, because it's a bunch of box-like houses right up next to the railroad. It was an accident, really. I told you earlier the planes missed the railroad and got the houses. A whole bunch of people died there. The second time they got the railroad, and the railroad was all on end after that.

What happened was, when the bomb came Denise went under the sink, and it came down and broke her pelvis, so she was in braces for a long time. She could hardly walk. Her mother was German, I think her father was in Germany. Denise was pretty, and after the war she met a Canadian guy. She said, "Deliver this letter for me." So she gave me a note to bring to the castle for the Canadian guy. Later she married him, too.

Nathalie's neighbor, that family from my aunt Sarah, they saw me by that Canadian guy talking. I told him what Denise said to me. I gave the envelope to him and came back. As soon as I came back, Fredric was standing there. He said, "I know what you was doing. I know you was chasing the soldiers." Oh my God, I got a beating. I got more beatings than food in my life, I tell you.

CHAPTER TWENTY-ONE

WHO THE HELL IS THE CRIMINAL HERE? HIM OR ME?

JENNY WAS A HEAVY DUTY GIRL. SHE LOVED FOOD. SHE WOULD do everything for food. My mother and Jenny were working together at the weaving mill until around eleven at night, while I watched the kids. A guy was working there in the weaving mill, and he took Jenny out to dinner, I guess. It was a long dinner. She had a child from him. When Erwin came loose from prison, he accepted that. The family didn't. They thought it was horrible. Erwin said, "Well, the war brought us trouble. I couldn't provide for her." They named her Melanie, and he raised the kid like it was his own, and he never said a word about it. That's the way he was. Erwin spoiled those kids, too. I don't know too much about Melanie, because I was then already on the leaving side.

We moved out of Jenny's house when Erwin came home. We stayed with my grandmother in that little house until my mother found something. I was still working at the weaving mill because I had to pay for the food. I got different jobs. My mother didn't have any income from Geoff. We were not long there when Geoff came back. I think he got amnesty. The king, Baudouin, he let everybody go, but they stripped them of their citizenship, and they took their voting away. I don't know exactly what it was, but my mother told me that. That is when we moved back in that house in Ghent.

When Geoff came home for good, that's when the problems started.

When you met him, he was always nice. But under that laughing there was an ugly place.

Right away his behavior changed toward me when he got out of prison. It didn't take much to wind him up. He was okay for a little while, but then my mother could never go to her family, and we had to go wherever he wanted, to the park and nonsense things like he wanted to go to a junk yard. I didn't want to go to a dumb junk yard. When we didn't listen to him, then he turned around and he hit the walls, and this and that.

Because my mother was with the kids, and I was young, he thought he could do anything that he wanted with me like my mother. Remember, in his mind he was still with the S.S. in Poland and Yugoslavia, and the German soldiers beat and raped anyone they wanted. He thought in Belgium he could do that to me, too.

The apartment building was a three-story place, and we lived at the top. The other people that lived there, they had the same type of room, but they was nice and clean. Not ours. We only had one room. Antoine slept on some little thing in the coal room. My mother got a bed, and in the middle was my little brother, Simon, the baby, and I had the other part with my sister. Geoff hung potato sacks between the beds. There was a table and some chairs and a big pot stove we cooked on. That was it. Then we had to go downstairs to pee, or we had to pee in a pot and we dumped it down there.

I slept with my sister, and during the night Geoff slipped in and tried to lay down next to me. I kicked him off. My mother woke up and we had a big battle. He said to her, "I'm looking at my daughter." Sure he was.

My mother was not stupid. She said to me, "What do you always have to start yelling for?" The next night he tried it again, and the next night after that. A few times I hit him. Geoff got pissed off, and he would hit me, my mother would scream and yell, the neighbors would come to the door and say, "Hey, can you please quiet down."

Geoff said, "Well, it is her fault."

Sure it was my fault, because I didn't want to take my pants off for him.

Most of the time I got stuff from other people. They said, "Take my bike." Geoff started following me all the time from the mill on his bicycle. He was a sneaky son of the gun. He knew the way so good. So I was on the bike riding and he came out on his bike, and he hit me, "Boom" and I fell off onto the street. Somewhere the guy from the company saw that happen, so he came with the car from the company. Then Geoff split. The guy from the company picked me up, took me to the nurse, and dressed my leg up. When I went home, my mother said, "What happened to your leg?"

Geoff sat there and looked at me. I told her the truth, exactly, and he said, "Me? I couldn't do that!" He said, "No! Was not me!"

The boss from the company told me, "What the hell are you doing with the guy?"

I said, "I don't know. That's my stepfather."

I couldn't sleep while I was home, because Geoff was always messing around on the bed. I was so tired the boss let me sleep in his office. I told the boss, "I can not handle him."

"Well, I'll bring you out to the bicycle when you leave and watch for him," he said.

Once in a while I came home, and Geoff would not be there, and my mother said, "Geoff saw that the boss helped you all the way to your bicycle, and he kissed you, and he saw that."

I don't let the boss kiss me. He made it up, I guess.

I said, "So? That's his problem."

"Well," she said, "You cannot do that. You are too young."

I said, "No. I have to work for you, and I have to protect myself." I didn't say, "from him." I didn't want to hurt my mother's feelings, so I kept to myself.

Geoff hit my mother all the time. I told her, "Why can't you just say nothing?"

"I can't."

I said. "Yes, you can! Put a cloth in your mouth or something. Because every time you say something, he will beat you, you know, and the kids." I said to my mother, "Stand up to him!" I was working the night shift and I went to the cinema and made some extra money. I told her to keep the money under the table, that he don't know. So she told him where the damn money was. I said, "Why do you tell him? It's not his money! I worked for that money."

My mother said, "Oh, but he would hit me."

I said, "Hit him back! Then he wouldn't hit you no more."

"No, because a woman won't do that."

Well, I did one time. There was a little storage closet where we put wood, and coal and whatever. We don't have showers, so I had to use a bucket. I was in there and I washed myself. Then he opened the door and he said to my mother, "I have to wash her back."

I screamed. I said to my mother, "If he comes in here, I'll break his—" Oh my God, you wouldn't believe what I said to him. But the Lord saved me anyway.

My mother said, "Why can't he wash your back?"

I don't understand her. I think she lost it.

I said, "All I want to do is get out of here."

Then I left, and Geoff followed me down the street.

In a little town like that, the whole neighborhood knew what was going on. Everybody knew he was S.S. when he came back. They said to me, "Rachel, get out of there."

There was a guy there, two houses down, and he had a little café where we could go and play billiards. They made money there, because in Belgium all they do is drinking. The owner was a world champion boxer, George de Wile, and everybody knew him. He was a guy that in the neighborhood lived. George was tiny, and he could fight. I didn't know him at that moment, but he was in the street and saw me and he said, "Where are you running to?"

I said, "From my stepfather."

"Come in!" said he, "Go to the basement." So I went in there as fast as I could go and sat down behind the beer can, and said, "Oh, thank you, Lord, for saving my life!" When I went along the side street to George's café, Geoff would lose me.

Later George called me where I worked and said, "Can we meet?" He told me he was wrestling so-and-so and gave me tickets, because they cost money, you know. I didn't care for it either. I never liked boxing, and I never liked wrestling, but every time I felt unsafe, or when Geoff was looking for me, and I saw him sneaking around with his hat pulled over his eyes, then George was close. One, two houses down, boom, I'm in, and I went down to his basement. As soon as other people got involved, Geoff stopped and went back to my mother like an angel.

A lady across the street had an ice cream and pastry store, and she was a sweetheart. When we moved into a street like that, most sometimes is a bakery, is a meat store, is a bar. She always stood in the doorway and saw me coming out of the house, so she knew exactly what happened. She told me, "When he's chasing you, run in the store." But then I had to go across the street, and that scared me because of the traffic. But one time I did run to her. It was hard because Geoff saw me cross the street and knew I was there and waited outside. She had to call the cops. I loved to go by her, but he would know what I was doing.

Sometimes Charles got me a room. Charles would sneaky, tell me, "Go to the hotel," and he would pay. Then I could stay by myself and sleep. I didn't need much, just a bath and sleep that nobody could bother me.

So many people were there to help me at the last moment. I was so thankful. The funny part was, when people let me sleep in their houses for a night, then Geoff would tell the family, "Oh yeah, she's a prostitute."

My uncles said, "Are you sure about that?" They knew better.

One time, my mother and Geoff got in a fight, and he hit her. She flew back over the couch. I took the iron poker and hit him right in the crotch. He lay on the floor and crawled like a worm. I told him, "If you touch me again, you're dead." My mother stood up and saw him rolling on the floor, and she came to me and slapped me around. I ran away again that night to a hotel room. He couldn't pee for a few days after that. I came back later. Not right away, believe me. But I could not stay away. I was still underage, and I didn't have a passport.

I wasn't afraid so much that Geoff would rape me, but I was afraid that when he grabbed me, I would knock him down and kill him.

Charles said, "Don't do nothing to that guy, because you're going to suffer for it."

I said to Charles, "Who the hell is the criminal here? Him or me?"

"Well," he said, "Remember, he still has a lot of German friends." After the S.S. was defeated, they always stuck together, so you had to be careful.

I said, "Yeah. That is for darn sure."

Charles said, "Next time you go over and he starts trying to crawl into the bed, go right away to the police department." In Europe it's stupid. You can't go to the cops, because they don't want to get involved in family issues. So long as I don't have a passport, I could not leave my mother.

After I hit Geoff with the poker he was scared of me. He still tried to hit me with the bike a few times, but he never got too close to me again.

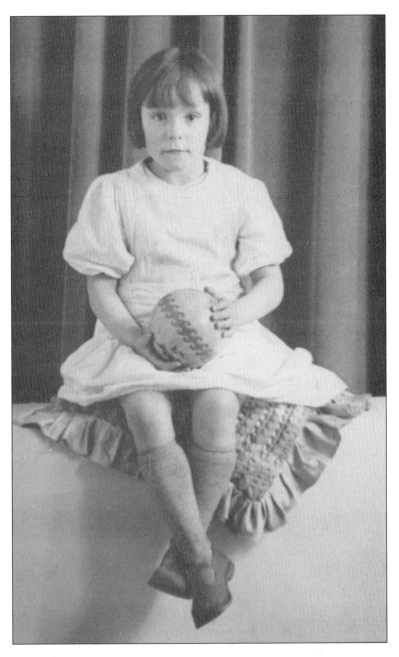

Rachel's picture taken on her seventh birthday, after Aunt Jenny had her hair cut, described in chapter 8. On the back the photo is stamped, "6 Oct. 1936."

left: Rachel's mother. On the back the photo is stamped "Studio Rapid Korte Munt 6 Jan. 1940. (Koornmarkt) Gent." Rachel says it was taken shortly before her mother joined the S.S.

below: Rachel with her mother. This is the doll photograph described in chapter 1.

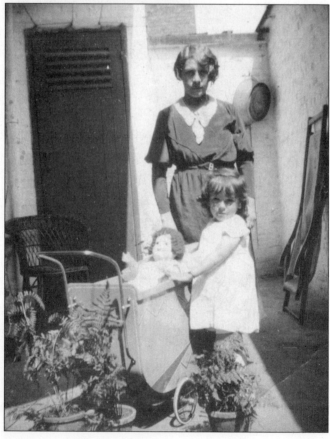

right: Rachel standing with her grandfather, 1937. You can see the row of apartments where she grew up in the background.

below: From left to right: (back row) Rachel's mother, Rachel's grandfather, Rachel's Aunt Jenny (in this picture she was still in training to be a nun), (front row) Rachel, Rachel's grandmother, Rachel's Aunt Sofie.

Rachel's grandfather and grandmother

Rachel's mother

From left to right: Aunt Jenny, Rachel's mother (sitting), Aunt Sofie.

From left to right: Fredric, Edmond (sitting), Michiel.

The wedding picture: Alfred Caluwaerts with Rachel's mother. Described in chapter 5.

above: The classroom of the Catholic school, as described in chapter 4. Rachel is sitting on the second row from the front on the right column. She is the girl on the left end of the desk. She believes the girl in the very back of the class wearing the ribbon in her hair, center right column, is Aurelie, the girl who was hit by the tram in chapter 4.

right: Rachel, in her confirmation photograph.

Lud's father, John, after his liberation from the Japanese POW camp. On the back is written, "Manilla, Oct 10th 1945. Pr. Sgt. No 53410. Comp. bbo. Platoon 2. Tent 20. Liberated Personnel. Section A.P.O. 711. Inter Island. Manilla."

above: Rachel and Lud's wedding picture, August 8, 1954. In the back, from left to right, Daisy, Lud's youngest sister, and Lud's oldest sister, Evadne. Much further back, you can see Leo Rasso.

right: Rachel with her first baby.

The front door of the house where Rachel's mother was taken by the resistance. This picture was taken years later, but if you look closely you will see that the door has been painted over where the resistance put the swastika.

CHAPTER TWENTY-TWO

I WANT TO STAND ON MY OWN FEET, AND I WILL

ONE NIGHT I CAME HOME FROM THE FLOSS COMPANY ON A BIKE. It was real dark, and Geoff was hiding behind the door. I came in and he grabbed me, pushed me against the wall, and tried to undress me. Well, I clawed and kicked and bit him. He pinned his knee between my legs so I couldn't move. I yelled and I screamed, and the neighbors downstairs ran up. The neighbor opened the door, and Geoff split. In the back is a toilet, and he ran to the toilet, so nobody could see him. But the neighbors knew.

I left everything there and I left, and I was on the street. At that moment I was so in pain, because I always had to fight. At that moment I couldn't think. I was so upset, I wanted to end my life. I really did. But then again, something stopped me and said, "No, no, no, no, that's not the way to go." There has to be somewhere, there is always somebody that can pick you up.

I ran to the police and sat there shaking. It was the first time I got the commissar to talk to me. He sat down with me and he said, "I want to know what's going on here." I was tired, so he said, "You know what? I'll put you in a little room where you can relax."

I said, "Call Dr. Charles Allary."

He said, "Okay, I will talk to him." So he did, and he came back. I was sound asleep, and he said, "Okay, I'll bring you some coffee, and we're going to talk." He brought me some coffee and we talked and talked. He said, "Listen, stay here, and I'll watch you. Tomorrow Charles is going to talk to another person who is going to have a job for you." That's the way it went.

The next day, Charles sent me to Gerard Vander Putten for a job. He was the chief of the employment agency in Ghent. You had to bring papers in when you had a job that said who your mother was, who your father was, where you was born, what classes you did, what school you did, graduation. I didn't have all my papers. I had a mother. That's as far as I could go. I didn't finish my school. I couldn't tell them, "My stepfather's S.S., my mother's S.S." Nobody's going to hire you for a maid, and certainly not for a nanny, when your mother and father were S.S. Gerard had to go and get me papers, and when something went wrong, he would step in and help me. I asked him, "What is available?"

He said, "Well, you can do this and this, but you cannot do this and this." I had to take the jobs that was easier on me. So he gave me a list of addresses and I walked to all the houses.

There were two sisters and a brother, and they needed a maid to do all the work, because they were all in their seventies and eighties. The brother's name was Mr. Francois. He was a widower, and the two sisters were widows. The oldest sister, Madam Marie, sat with me in the front room, and she was alone with me, and she watched me, my attitude. That was important, how you acted. I learned that from Charles. Then she asked me questions, and she said, "Well, I'm going to try you out first, and see how you are." I don't know what Gerard told her, but I couldn't cook. I could take care of the kids, but we didn't have all the rooms and luxury.

The old people talked French, so I knew they had money. When people spoke the Flemish dialect like mine, then you knew they were from lower class.

The house was beautiful. There was a little marble hallway, the salon, a big, huge room, another room where the table and chairs sat, then the kitchen with a big stove. I had my own little room upstairs in the attic. It was nice. Simple, but it was better than what I got at my mother's. I had nothing then.

I had to wear a maid's uniform, a black dress with a stiff white collar, white sleeves, and white apron. At dinner, I wore long sleeves, because they didn't want me to serve with open arms.

They were rich people, so I didn't know too much about them. Here in America you can ask anybody anything, but in Europe when they were richer than us, you said, "Thank you" for everything and just did what they told us.

Both sisters were gray, and they picked their hair up with some pins. Their spouses hadn't died recently, but they were always in black. Everyday they wore black shoes, black socks, black blouses, black slippers. Except they always had a white collar on, like nuns. How funny is that.

The youngest sister was buckled and walked hunched over. Once in a while she would look up, you know. She was with her son in France before she came to Belgium. She was a nice person, but she couldn't straighten. She sat always in a special chair in the salon with her books. When she sat down, then I could see her face. She looked hard, frowning. But when I sat down and talked to her, I liked her. She was really pretty nice.

She did a lot of paperwork. I'm not sure if it was for her, or her son, or for the money in whatever business Mr. Francois owned. He slept in a separate room. The two sisters slept in one room in different beds. The youngest sister had a special cushion she used when she slept. When they came down for breakfast, then I went up, opened the beds so they are airing, and then I came back down and helped them out.

Mr. Francois owned a factory, but I really don't know what factory it was. He had money, that's for sure. His grandson always came by him and helped his grandfather. Madam Marie told me that his daughter went to Argentina and she died on a plane crash. So he took care of the kids, I think. His wife died when she was giving birth. They put the kids in a special school. He would tell me that his daughter died, that he had to take care of the boy, but that was it. He was heavier than his sisters and moved real slowly. I had to give him his slippers and I took his shoes in the kitchen, cleaned them up, and put them on the stairs. Then he took them, and I made his bed, things like that. All the work they couldn't do I did for them.

He said, "Hi," "Good morning," but most of the time he would go in the salon, close the door, and the only communication I had with him is when I served the table. He read the newspaper, and he was always reading the financial page. I came in with the coffee in the afternoon and he lay there snoring. He could be in the grave. No difference. Once in a while when he had big company over for dinner, he would have a cigar. But that was seldom.

Madam Marie was pretty nice to me. She was tall and gray, and really slender. She always helped me with telling me what to do, and what they said. They had a wood stove, and once in awhile Madam Marie would sit there and she watched me while I cleaned the stove, and she asked me questions. I told her, "You have such beautiful color and hands." For her age she looked really good.

Then she said, "Oh, that's because I come from France," and she was really well taken care of. She told me a little bit about that. She worked in France, but then she got a sickness, and her son thought, "Oh, you were better off with your brother and your sister." So he sent her back to Belgium.

She taught me to cook, but not fancy dishes. Always potatoes and vegetables, and everything was cooked dead, mashed, because they couldn't bite too good, I guess.

Every day she called in, and the baker came, and the meat, and whatever she ordered I had to make. In the morning it was always the same. They had to have a poached egg in a little egg cup in the morning with jam and toast with apples. The boss wanted coffee. The girls wanted tea, and later, around ten o'clock, I got them coffee. At three o'clock, I went in with more coffee, and sometimes one wanted a cookie, or maybe a piece of pie or chocolate. The big meal was at noon and began with soup. They always had soup. Sometimes they had a little toast with mushrooms. Then after that, they had always a rice pudding or prune juice. The pudding I made. The pies they made themselves. Madam Marie did some cooking, and the pies were tiny, not like American pies.

I think they had a good education because they were rich. Madam Marie said to me, "Go to the library," and she wrote down what to pick up, and I went and got the book. She told me, "Okay, I'm going to sit with you, and I read, and you write." So we sat in the kitchen and did as much I could, and then I went back to the library and brought some more books.

I heard them laughing and talking to each other in French, so I didn't understand it. I didn't keep up with French. They spoke French to me, and they knew I couldn't answer, so they were real gentle with me, and they taught me slowly. French addressed ladies and gentlemen as, "Madam" and "Monsieur." To a girl you said "Mademoiselle." You never call them by their first name. I always called them Madam so-and-so.

They were Catholic, and the priest came by them all the time.

He brought the communion, and he talked to them, and then the door would be locked.

In the morning, I came down and put the stove on. They were dressed up when they came down. I beat the carpets and polished the stove once a week, but I did everyday vacuum.

I remember my brother Antoine, who was then four years old, and my sister Sarah, who was six, came over asking for money. Between the doors in their house was a foyer. Madam Marie took me in there and she said, "Don't give them money. Just pay the bill for the grocer." She said, "Otherwise they are going to take the money and don't pay it back."

So I told them that I wouldn't give them money. "Whatever you want, I'm going to go and pay the baker." Madam Marie said, "Here's your money, but I'm going to hold it for you." She said, "By the way, you have no clothes." She bought that uniform for me, and that's all I had. The clothes from Charles were fancier clothes, and I could not wear them working. She said, "And you need clothes." I bought a jacket. I didn't have a skirt and a blouse, and she was mad about that. She said, "No, you have to take care of yourself."

I tried to go to school during that time. They had classes for adults in the evening after dinner, around seven o'clock. Madam Marie said to me, "Pick up your writing and your reading." I'm still pretty good at reading, but not writing, because it's such a mixed language.

I did a few classes, and I think Geoff found out. I didn't tell anyone where I was working, but he found me, believe me, he did.

The school was not that far away from where I worked. There was a big park there with statues, the Kaisers this, the Kaisers that. I went from the house, across the park, and on the corner is another house, and next to the house is the school. But somehow Geoff was watching me, I guess, and he knew I went through the park. So one day I came back across the park, and there he came with his bicycle. "Poom!" The ground was gravel, and there I lay. I went home to Madam Marie, and I cleaned up. After that I couldn't go back to school no more, because I knew Geoff would follow me again. Then he started spreading rumors about me and the teacher and the students. Nobody talked to me or they would sleep with me. So I stopped going to school.

Charles took me out. He said to me, "We're going to drive out, and I have to talk to you." When they say "out" they mean "out of Ghent."

I said, "Okay." So I got ready and I had some things done, then he picked me up somewhere, and then we drove out. He said, "I'm getting married. My parents want that." He said, "You know, they bug me and bug me." He didn't want to get married, but he was getting older and older and in Europe most of the time people married friends from the parents. Why it is like that, I have no idea. Here in America you look for your own bride, not your mother. In Europe when you is a girl, the father looks for your husband.

We ate, then I got a cup of coffee and he said, "I have something for you." He said, "Look, I made up a list. I think, because I did so much for you, I cannot dump you. So, what I want to do is, I want to get you an apartment. That is with everything in it, the furniture, and I pay for it. I put the money in the bank, and you take it out and pay all the bills and whatever you want."

So I looked at the list, and it said he would do that apartment; he would do the clothes like we always did, because the clothes were expensive, and the food was for me. Plus whenever he could he would call me and then we would go out. And that was the point. I said to him, "What makes you think I want to do that? See, the clothes won't go, because I'm not going to accept that. That food's not going, because I won't accept that. And the apartment certainly isn't going to go. You are married."

He said, "What do we do then?"

I said, "Then we say goodbye. That's it."

He said. "I cannot do that. After all that I did for you?"

I said, "Yeah. After all you did for me. Because," I said to him, "There is a price."

He said, "That's not going to happen. You're not free from your mother and you need my help." And that was true.

They always said, "You're going to become like your mother." They said, "You're going to have bastards like your mother." And those two things already I said, "Ho ho! That's not going to happen!" And I fought like hell so that it didn't. And I had the personality to do that. I was not selling myself. It was not easy, but I did. I didn't want to be like my mother, and I never was like my mother. You know what they called them? "Madams." I didn't want to be a madam either.

"Okay," I told him, "You can help me. When you want to take me to dinner, that's okay. I'm hungry. I'll eat. But I'm not going to go out with you, and I'm not taking an apartment. Then I wouldn't be the same. Stupid like my mother. I want to stand on my own feet. And I will."

CHAPTER TWENTY-THREE

WHAT THE HELL HAPPENED NOW?

MOST OF THE TIME ON MY DAY OFF I WOULD GO IN THE MORN-ing to church and put the candles on. I had money to pay for the seat, and I sat and talked to the Lord, thanked Him for what He did for me, thanked Him for everything, asked Him to help me. I didn't talk to Mary, I didn't talk to Joseph. I went right to the cross. Maybe it was not right, but that's the way I did it.

There was a monk. Sometimes he came and asked if I wanted communion.

I said, "No. I don't want to do that."

He said, "You want to talk? You can ask questions. You can ask any questions." He asked me why I didn't come to mass.

I told him I was not welcome.

He looked at me, and he said, "Who says so?"

I said, "Well, I'm going to tell you who says so. That priest who did my confirmation."

He said, "No!"

I said, "Yeah." Then I explained why. I framed exactly what happened. I told him, "I am a bastard, and I am no good," because that's what people told me all the time.

Then I saw in his face, you know, he was not comfortable with what I asked him, because he didn't know exactly how to answer to my question, see. He didn't know why I didn't have the Missal, and then he thought there had to be something wrong with me, otherwise I would have the Missal. He said, "No, they can't do that."

I said, "No, but they did. What other reason could there be for not giving me the book?"

The monk looked at me and said, "Well, that is your thinking, but I don't think that was the reason."

Sometimes I went to see my mother. Sometimes I was scared. I did love my mother, but I could not stand Geoff. So it was to me a fight to go to her. But then again I did.

I helped her out to pay the bills, but it was not good for me to do that because every time I got her food, Geoff went and spent money in the bars and wherever he went. I think the government gave them something. Because of his eyes, he was disabled to work. That's what he told them. He was not blind to chase women, he was not blind to drink beer, so I wonder if he was blind or not.

I wouldn't come in when Geoff was there. Are you kidding me? And he wouldn't allow her out of the house without him. Geoff wouldn't go anywhere without that bicycle. So if I went by there and saw the bicycle gone, then I went in.

Physically she was a wreck. She played cards, cards, cards. She didn't want to do nothing. When you asked her something, she said, "I don't know," and "I don't want to know." She hated religion. They all still believed Hitler would be on the top, and Hitler would do this, and Hitler would do that. It was all Hitler. God was not even on her mind.

I didn't see my mother much, unless she asked me to come over and do something, or my sister came over and asked me for money.

Whenever I went over to my mother's house, then I put old clothes on. If they saw my nice clothes, they wanted more money. When I was working or shopping, then I had to have good clothes on. Always a dress, because they didn't believe in pants for women in Europe at that time. You had one dress, then you could have three or four blouses. But when I was working for the Francoises, once in awhile my mother asked where I got my clothes.

Geoff told my mother that I was sleeping with this guy and I was sleeping with that guy, and my mother believed that. "Who got you that? Who gave you that?"

Finally I said, "Well, I bought it myself." I asked her, "Why ask me that? I'm working."

She said, "Geoff came home and told me that he saw you going out with so and so and so."

I said, "So what? I don't sleep with him."

I was probably between seventeen and eighteen. It was real hot. That was unusual in Europe. Some cousins from my aunt Marie said, "We're going to go to the river. Do you want to go?"

So I went with them. When I was in the water, instantly I felt numb in my legs and I couldn't move no more. The guys saw me going down, and they thought I was playing. So finally they saw that I couldn't move, and the guy jumped in, got me out, and lay me down. So they brought me to the hospital, and a nurse took care of me until Charles came. Then they found out it was my appendix blown open, so they operated right away. After I just came out of the hospital from my appendix operation, my sister cried and she said, "Mom wants you to come."

I said, "Okay." So I went. Geoff was not there. I don't know where the hell he was.

My brother was playing marbles, and I think they rolled under the bed. So he took some matches, I guess, and got down to look under the bed. He was a clever guy. The whole thing went up, and with those potato sacks hanging, it smoked like hell, and stunk.

My mother was on the toilet downstairs. I was talking to her, and then I looked up and there was smoke coming out. I said "What are you cooking?"

She said, "Nothing."

I said, "Well, something's smoking."

In the meantime I heard the kids, my sister and Antoine, running down the stairs. We ran up and Simon lay there in the crib, and the crib was burning. My mother took the radio, and she ran out with the radio. I looked at her, and I thought, "Are you stupid or what?" I said, "What do you take the radio for?"

She said, "That is not paid for."

I said, "Well, nothing is paid for in that place." So I took the kid.

In the meantime the fire department was already there. I had the baby. They had to help him. He couldn't breathe because there was a lousy carpet around the crib and it was smoking like hell. Lucky the fire department helped me, because he saw blood coming out my blouse, and he said, "What happened? Are you bleeding?"

I said, "No, what would I be bleeding for?" I didn't even feel that appendix incision came open. So I had to go back in, and they closed it again. There was some fluid in the stomach, and they put a tube in there to clean it out.

Antoine said later, "The whole family called me the fire maker." In Belgium when you do something wrong, you are stamped forever.

The war was over, but my mother didn't have a job. Geoff didn't have a job. They didn't give him a job, or he didn't go for a job, I don't know. But at that moment, there was a lot of people still going to court, sitting in jail, and all this stuff.

A court server brought papers to the house from Geoff. Well, I had to sign for it. Madam Marie said, "Can I see it?" So I gave it to her, because I was working in her house. I could be a criminal or something, and she had the right to know that. But I knew better, that it was for something else. After she read the papers, she called her lawyer. She told me not to worry about it. She said, "Everything is taken care of."

I said, "Okay."

So I had to go in to court again. I saw Geoff walking the hallways. He couldn't come in. He had that cap pulled down over his eyes. The French people did that, put their hats on crooked, and then you know they're up to something.

I thought, "What the hell happened now?" With him you never knew. Always surprises, you know. I went in and my mother was there. My mother always whispered to me. She was scared from the guy. She said, "I have to come. I have to bring you here."

I said, "For what? What did I do?"

She said, "I sent the papers in for your salary."

I wasn't making that much. 800 francs. I said, "What do you want my salary for? That's your husband. He makes kids. When he makes kids, then he can work, too."

There was a lady judge. The lawyer wasn't there, but he had already talked to the judge. So they had the papers, and the judge asked my mother, "You want her money?"

She said, "Yeah."

The judge said, "For what? She's not even living with you. She's working for the Francoises."

"Yeah," she said, "But I want her salary."

The judge said, "You don't do nothing for her. And, by the way," she said, "Here's the papers. You signed her away to a German camp."

My mother said, "Yeah, well, I had to for my husband."

The judge said, "It's not even your husband. You're not even married with him. Why do you want her money?"

She said, "Because he's not working."

Afterwards, the judge told me to go and get a passport because I was too constrained by that. I couldn't get a passport until I was twenty-one, but what they did give me was a work permit with my picture on it. So they knew who I was and what I did.

Geoff was pissed. The balconies of the Francois's house had windows on the side, and from them you could see the front entrance. So one night Madam Marie saw Geoff drop something in the mailbox. In the morning she said, "There's something in the mailbox. Somebody dropped it in." She didn't want to say it was him.

When I took it out and I read it, he said scary things about what was going to happen to me, what he was going to do to me, and he said, "From the Black Mask."

She said, "Is it nice?"

I said, "Here it is," and she read it. She called the police, and the police came, she gave them the note, and away was the note. I didn't see Geoff around there no more.

The lawyer told Madam Marie, "It's better for her to get away from here, because that guy is not going to leave her alone."

Charles told me he would check it out in Antwerp and find something for me there.

I could not make the old people suffer for my mother's mistakes. I sat down with Madam Marie, and we talked, and I explained that I was going to quit there because I wanted to go to Antwerp. They helped me a lot, and I felt sorry for everything they did for me. She was okay with it. She knew the pain I went through, she knew about my sister and my brother coming to the house asking for money, and she knew that I did not lie about it, so she said, "Well, what is best for you?" Then she told me I could go back to her anytime I wanted, and that was the end of it.

CHAPTER TWENTY-FOUR

IT WAS NICE SEEING YOU

I MIGHT BE POOR, AND I MIGHT BE UGLY, BUT NOBODY MESSED around with me, I tell you that.

A couple of days later, I got a job with a salesman who went to Switzerland to pick up tools, like doctor's knives for operations in the hospital. He was an ugly German guy. Oh, was he ugly. When he was gone, I took care of the kids and the house. His wife's name was Vasse. She was good-looking for her age, by the way, a beautiful body and hands. They used her for modeling in a painting academy. She had two kids from him. Ugly kids at that. She took him maybe for the money. I don't know what she took him for. Anyways, they lived in an apartment, and she got hurt or something and walked with a limp, so she couldn't take care of the kids.

At night I worked for a nice older lady who owned a big huge waffle house. They called her Maxine. My mother knew her for awhile and stayed with her when she was pregnant with me. I don't know what happened there because I was not born yet, but my mother asked her if she wanted to be my godmother, and she said "Yes." Her husband had died in the war. I have a feeling he was Jewish, so I think the Germans took him, and he never came back. She had one son, and he was in the soldiers, and I think he died, too. But she was rich, believe me.

I asked her, "Do you have some job for me?"

They had a big huge bar with glasses, and she said, "Do you mind? When we close down," and that was sometimes four o'clock in the morning, "Then you can wash all the glasses and the sink and everything." I did that for extra money. So she took care of me at a time that I needed her. I didn't sleep, either. Believe me, I couldn't. I had to make money, and it was not easy.

During that time Charles and I were sitting in a restaurant, and a man walked in. Charles said, "Oh, Arthur!" and the man came over and he sat down, and they had a cup of coffee. They were both friends. They worked together in college or school, I don't know. They were always high society, and most of the time they all gathered together. He was tall and blond, blue-eyed, a real beautiful guy. They had a lot of money. I didn't, you know. And he looked at me and looked at me and looked at me, and then he said to Charles, "Who's that lady?"

Charles told him about me.

Then he said, "Oh, okay."

Then later I bet Charles thought that Arthur could help me, so he told Arthur, "Check out what she's doing."

Arthur found out where I worked. He called and he said to me, "I want to talk to you."

I said, "What do you want to talk to me for?"

"Well," he said, "Gerard Vander Putten told me there was troubles that you needed a job or something."

I said, "Yeah, I do have problems." So then we sat down in my room, I had my own room, and I told Arthur all about it. We talked and talked, and I told him that I needed paper work done. Anybody that could help me, I said, "Thank you."

He said, "Oh, that's the case." At that moment we just talked and he went away. Later on he called me back and he always came to the waffle house where I was working and said, "I'll pick you up. I want to go there with you and get some coffee, some snacks, whatever."

He was much older than me. He never talked about himself, but he was nice and charming. The newspapers were always chasing him with cameras, so whatever he did he had to do it behind closed doors. So most of the time we were out of town, or he would put on something so nobody recognized him.

One time when we went out for dinner, we were driving and driving, and I thought, "Where are we going?" We were driving so far I thought, "I'm never going to come back."

He said, "Let's go to Paris."

I thought, "No. That's too far. I'm not safe there."

He said, "Well, nobody will know."

Something told me, "Uhn uh, that's not right," because I was scared something would happen. I didn't really know Arthur that good, either. He was a nice friend and he helped me. Charles was different. Charles I knew for years, you know. But I just knew Arthur through Charles, that's it. So I said, "No, I'm staying here, and you go to Paris."

So he dropped me off somewhere, and I went back with the streetcar, and he went to Paris. Lucky I was not with him. He was walking in Paris, somebody hit him with a car, and broke his arm. It was all over the newspapers.

So I said to Charles, "Something told me not to go."

Later at the waffle house my godmother told me, "You know who Arthur is?"

I said, "No."

She said, "He's the mayor's chauffer. I have a picture of him."

So then I saw him in the picture with his wife and two daughters. I didn't know that, because he never talked about it.

I told him, "I'd rather not communicate with you, because I don't want to be in the newspapers. I'd be the boo boo girl and you'd be the good Samaritan." In Belgium at that time when somebody is high society and you are low class, you are the one that is bad. For me, I always had a thing on my forehead that I was a bastard. I didn't need to be a whore, too. They could destroy me like that. I didn't trust nobody. I was underage, and they were all big men, and I was really not ready for all this.

Arthur said, "Charles is going to get married. What are you going to do?"

I said, "Nothing." Was hard on me, though. I didn't know what to do, really.

So Arthur said to me, "Shall I get you an apartment?"

I said, "No. Because I know what is going to happen." I told him. "I want to be free. Not somebody else's puppet."

And he said to me, "You don't have to."

I said, "Yes, I have to. Because when Charles gives me an apartment, when you give me an apartment, that's not because you like me. That is because there's a giving and a taking here."

There were a lot of wolves in Belgium. Well, hey, Belgium, France, you have them all over the place. When I told Charles about Arthur, he told me, "This never happened before."

I asked Charles, "What shall I do?"

He said, "Well, don't go into this, because he's married, too."

I said, "Yes, they told me."

He said, "Tell him to knock it off, because you're going to have a problem here."

So I said, "Oh, okay." And I didn't have to, the Lord took care of it.

On the first of the month, Vasse owed me 800 francs. Is not much, by the way. She knew I needed people to help me to get another job, so she said, "I don't have the money. My husband is not back from Switzerland yet, and when he comes back, then I pay you."

I said, "No, I need my money now. The month is over."

She said, "Well, you have to wait."

"Oh no," I told her, "You pay me now, because you have money. I know you do, or I'm leaving."

"Where?"

I said, "Anywhere!"

"Where are you going to sleep?"

I said, "That is not your business either."

Arthur came over to pick me up for lunch or dinner or whatever. I went shopping, and I came back, and when I came in he was in the kitchen on a chair, and Vasse was sitting there in her negligee on his lap. That was it for me. He looked at me as if to say, "I'm innocent. She just did that." I looked at him, and I didn't say nothing. So I took my little suitcase and my little things that I got, not much clothes to put in there, and then she came after me and we fought. She said, "You're jealous from Arthur."

I said, "Give me a break. I'm not jealous from nobody. It's my money I want." I left, and she never did pay me.

Arthur was upset, and he said, "Wait! Wait!"

I walked out and went to the waffle house. I was sitting there, and then he came up and asked, "What did you walk out for? I didn't do nothing. It was not me. She crawled in my lap."

I didn't believe that. I said to Arthur, "Listen, you are a man. You know she is married, she has two kids. You don't allow that to happen."

He said to me, "I didn't do nothing! I just came in to pick you up!"

I said, "She didn't pay me, and I worked the whole month there."

He said, "Oh, that's what happened. She didn't tell me that."

I said, "Sure she's not going to tell you that."

So he said, "Okay, then I will pay you, then you will see that I'm sorry."

I don't go for bullshit like that. I'm a nice person, but when someone plays tricks on me like that, that's it. So when this all happened, it was okay with me, because it saved me from having to tell Arthur off. "It was nice seeing you." And that was the end for Arthur.

CHAPTER TWENTY-FIVE

IT'S TIME TO GET OUT OF HERE

I took my little things and my clothes, and I went to a taxi guy that I knew for a long time growing up. He had four or five limousines. Now they call them "limousines," but then they were "taxis." In the daytime I looked for jobs. In the nighttime when I didn't have no place to sleep I stayed in one of the cars. We sat down, and I asked the taxi driver, "What shall I do? This is what happened to me."

"Oh, there's somebody that I know," he said, "His name is Adrien and he needs somebody to take care of his kids. He owns the big Ford Company here. I'll take you there."

So I went with him, and they hired me.

Adrien was a tall, dark, good-looking guy in his thirties, black hair with a wave in it and clean hands. I always looked at a man's hands. The wife was always on the go with her sister-in-law to Paris, Greece, Spain, Italy, you name it, and they came back with beautiful French clothes. But they had money. She always left Adrien and the kids there alone.

Adrien's father was Jewish, and he was killed in the war, so his mother spent money like hell. She was heavy duty and gambled like crazy. Every day she went gambling there. Oh my God, she was something else. She had dark hair, all waves, bunched like a hotdog in the back with big pins. She wore beautiful stones in her hair, and she was always dressed to kill in a rich suit and beautiful blouses and furs with all this dazzling jewelry on her fingers. She had only ten fingers, and I think on every one of them was a ring. I was never crazy about jewelry or fur. I never said, "I wish I had that." I always told myself, "There is something wrong here that is not normal."

They had a big house, so I stayed there in a little room, and I took care of the kids. One was named Jolien, the other was Jean Pierre, a boy. The kids were pretty, too, really nice and they just behaved. The funny thing about it was the girl had hair like gold, and so did the boy. Maybe Adrien's wife painted her hair, I don't know. But Adrien was dark and she was dark, so somebody was lying here, you know. I liked the kids though. We sat outside, we talked, and we played games.

Sometimes when everybody went to bed, I did other things. I scrubbed the floors in the morning, and by the time I came back they were dry. They had some other help, too. One was a cook maid, because I was not a good cook. She was nice, but she had red hair. She came in the afternoon and stayed until about two o'clock getting all the pots and pans ready, and sometimes she made some stuff for the day after. She told me, "Rach, that is for tomorrow, so don't touch it." And then she left.

In the evening Adrien put the kids to sleep and stepped out. He liked to go out and see people and talk and drink and go to the Wednesday night wrestling matches. He took the cook to the wrestling matches for awhile. Later she got a boyfriend so he don't do that no more. He took me instead. I didn't like to drink. But once in awhile he would get me a liquor before dinner, and then we talked. He knew about my family, too, because it was all gone over when they hired me.

I didn't care for wrestling, either. He said, "Come on, we'll go out for dinner first." The dinner is what I went for. Afterwards at the wrestling arena, it was crowded with yelling and screaming and I sneaked out and sat at the bar and talked to the guy at the bar. After the match Adrien found me and said, "Where the hell were you?"

"At the bar," I said.

Then George de Wilde came in. He was fighting, and came over and hugged me. George was a big celebrity there. Ghent loved him.

Adrien looked at me, his eyes popping out. "You know him?"

I said, "Yeah, he's my neighbor."

"You're killing me!"

When I was there, I went with the kids to the park and there Geoff was, riding around on his bicycle. I was scared for the kids, so I said, "Oh shoot," you know. "I better get out of here." So I went back to Adrien's house, and I said, "Listen, that is what happened."

Adrien said, "You're kidding me."

I said, "No."

So he said, "Shall I send the cops after him?"

I said, "No. Because it is my stepfather, and I have to be careful for my mother." I could've called the police, too. But that's not what I wanted.

I quit with Adrien after maybe three weeks. Later I found out his company went bankrupt, because the mother always went gambling.

I called Madam Marie to help me, because she had told me, "So soon as you have problems, let me know," then she would help me with the lawyer. I phoned her, she phoned me, we were always in contact, you know. She then talked to the lawyer, called me, and she told me what to do. I had no money to hire a lawyer, so the people helped me like that.

We talked about it and she told me, "The lawyer said ask Charles to help you get out of here. Because Geoff is going to do that constantly. Wherever you work, that boy's going to find out where you are, and he's going to be there. He wants your money."

I went to Charles's office. I made out that I was sick so nobody knew. Then I was in his office, and then he talked to me. I said, "He's chasing me again. I have to do something. I'm going to kill this sucker because he don't leave me alone."

"Yes, it's time to get out of here," He said. "I'll make some arrangements in Antwerp, and I'll bring you to the bus, and I'll see that you are safe on the bus." So he said, "Hang in there. Don't go out too much with the kids. Don't do anything, and stay away from the parks." So I did. Later Charles called me back, and he said, "I found somebody in Antwerp. He's an inspector from Interpol. He's going to help you. And I know a lady, she's going to take care of you."

Charles got my tickets, he did everything for me, because he didn't want nobody to know. Then he said, "Tonight go to the bus station. I will be there."

In the meantime, I wanted to tell my mother. I told her, "Listen, I'm leaving." I didn't tell her where.

She said, "You can't. You have no passport."

I said, "No, I'm leaving anyway, so you don't going to see me no more."

She said, "You can't do that."

I said, "Yes I can." And then Geoff came in and we had a big fight again, and the neighbors were there, and the whole saboo. Then I left.

I told certain aunts that I was going to leave. And I went to Sofie, because she was always there when I was raised. I went in to the sanitarium and the nuns let me in. She came out, she had chains, and when the chains rattled, she was scared of them. She saw me and she remembered. So she hugged me, and then we sat down. The nun stood there watching, and Sofie whispered in my ear, "Can I have your lipstick?"

"Can you use lipstick here?"

She said, "Yeah, but I don't have any."

"Okay, you want it, then I give it to you." So I gave her my lipstick and my bag with everything in there. I don't know what she wanted with it, but she took that lipstick and put it on all over her mouth. The nun didn't say nothing. I showed her the mirror, and I thought I was going to die. I told her. "I'm going to leave. I'm not coming back for a long time."

She said, "Okay," and then she hugged me.

The last person I went to was my grandmother. She was all alone, laying in the bed. I said, "I'm going away, and I'm not coming back." She looked at me, and she turned away. I wanted to hug her, and she didn't like it. She was pissed off at me. I didn't tell her anything. I think she was already sick. That was the last time I ever saw her.

I had all my things in a bag, I climbed on a streetcar so nobody could see me, and when I came off, I saw Charles. He motioned for me to go into the station. I went into the building and looked around that nobody was there, then I went back out to his car, got my ticket, and he said, "And I'm staying here. Lay down till the bus comes by." So I laid in his car real close. The bus came, and I went in with the crowd and I jumped on the bus.

I told Charles, "I never want to come back. I'm never going to see you."

"That's okay. But don't forget to write, because I do want to have contact with you."

I said, "Okay." But later I heard he had a daughter, so the more I needed to stay away. I never interfered with his life. I did go back later and saw Charles, but I didn't know it at that moment, for the last time. He was still okay then, but I had a funny feeling that I was never going to see him again. He died after that. He died real young.

CHAPTER TWENTY-SIX

WHATEVER YOU WANT, I'LL DO FOR YOU

IT WAS LATE; THE LAST BUS TO ANTWERP. I DIDN'T TALK TO ANY-body. Antwerp is a big, huge port city, busy because all the guys came from the ships. It was like Paris a little bit. The business, the traffic, entertainment, and whatever was a lot bigger. At night the whole city lighted up and people always danced and drank.

When I came off the bus, Charles Kudler, a tiny, short and fat little man with a big nose, and a little bit jumpy, introduced him-self to me. He ran the restaurant from the brewery. He looked really Jewish, and when his mouth was open laughing, I could see his gold teeth.

I went with him in the car to the restaurant. He was a gentle-man. He said, "Oh, and we're going to have fun, and I like to see you, because I heard a lot about you, and we're going to be good, good friends."

I said, "I hope so, because I'm tired of jumping from place to place to place."

"No," he said, "My wife is going to love you."

I said, "Oh, okay. Thank you."

The restaurant was being leased to the Kudlers by a big brewery across town. It was a big place with two doors, and one was always open. Outside was a large window and it said "New York Bar." The inside was scattered all around with round tables, or you could sit at the bar in front. The glasses hung or stood behind the bar, and the kitchen was in the back.

Albertina Kudler had a beautiful face, dark like a gypsy with short hair, but she was three times as big as Charles was. She was from Ghent, and anyone from Ghent, they were outspoken. Sometimes too outspoken. We sat down, and we went over my story and everything that had happened to me. I could see she had a serial number stamped on her arm, and I thought, "What happened there?" We were stupid in these things. We didn't know what happened, you know. The war was not even cold yet.

She asked me, "Your mom was so-and-so."

I said, "Yes."

"Your stepfather was so-and-so."

I said, "Yes," and I thought to myself, "Uh oh, this is not going to work here."

"I have your room ready, and in the morning Inspector Beck is going to talk to you."

I said, "Oh, okay. Why?"

"Well," she said, "He has a message for you from a friend of yours in Ghent."

I thought, "Who the hell could that be?" Then I thought, "Uh oh, I have a feeling where it comes from."

Inspector Beck came in the morning because the restaurant didn't open until later. He was a big, huge Norwegian guy from Interpol across the street, in his sixties, and he spoke all the languages. He was not young, but he was tough. He had blond hair, it was not gray yet, and he had a big booming voice. He boarded all the ships that came in from Scandinavia and Ghent, and went over the notebooks, he checked the strangers out, who the sailors were, that they weren't fugitives or they weren't jumping ship. He was for years there, too.

He had always a brown hat on and a coat, and he came in and sat down. I had a cup of coffee, and he asked me questions about my mother and about my stepfather and about the war. So I told him the story. I'll never forget he looked right in my eyes, and I always looked away.

Charles knew there were a lot of bars there, so Charles sent a message to Inspector Beck, "Knowing her body, I know what's going to happen here. Somebody is going to take her."

Beck told me, "You're going to stay here, but I'm going to take care of you. Albertina's not. I am. So whatever happens, I will be in control. You cannot sit with people. You can serve. Don't let nobody touch you. Don't say nothing to people. Just serve and say 'thank you.' The people that come from the ships, you serve them. In the evening, you're going to be behind the bar that nobody can touch you."

The brewery was across town. They made a big ton of beer. Whenever we were empty and we needed beer, we called them and they brought new barrels. The barrels went into the basement with this big tap.

The time the restaurant opened every day had to do with the ships. Across the street was the Maritime Belge Company. The Kudlers knew that there was a lot of ships in when the Maritime Belge told them, and they opened early in the morning and served breakfast; coffee, sandwiches, boiled eggs, some garlic sausage, and lunch for the guys that were waiting for the ships to leave from Antwerp. They had little barrels with salt fish, too, and on the corner was a big lunch wagon. If the guys wanted French fries or special things that we didn't make in the restaurant, they said, "Oh, here's a franc," and one of us would run over to the lunch wagon and get French fries. Tina opened for maybe an hour, just to see how business was. When she liked it, and a lot of people came in, she stayed open. We could open early, we could close early, we could stay open longer. It was up to Tina. She didn't serve dinner. Well, there were a lot of restaurants. We gave them only breakfast.

The two other girls that worked at the restaurant, they had boyfriends that were sailors, and they sat with the guys drinking. They made money and went out sometimes for I don't know what. They were nice to me. They treated me like a little kid, and I was okay with that. One was Sonia. She was drunk as hell. She went to the store and bought gin. The other one was a nice dark haired girl named Jeanie. She didn't drink that much. She always made sure when she had drinks with the guys she baptized it, watered it down.

The bar opened up at night. Then I worked. Tina didn't pay me, because she gave me a free room upstairs, but I got to keep the money from the tips. I cleaned for her, and I did all the glasses and the silverware. That's the way it went, and she closed the restaurant at around 11 pm.

Tina said, "We're going to go shopping. I'm going to get you clothes."

I said, "Okay."

She asked me if I liked dresses.

I told her, "No. I like pants." Because I was safer with the pants.

"Well," she said, "But we have dresses here."

I said, "Yeah, I know. But do you mind that I have a long one then?"

"Oh no," she said. "That's okay."

So she went with me to her sister on a Friday, and her sister owned a big clothes store. We went in, and at that moment she paid for the clothes. I had to pay her back. Was not for free, I tell you that.

At first I was awful cautious. I was always scared from people, because they were strangers and I never knew what they were going to do to me. I was young, you know, and there were guys from all the ships, and they liked to touch. Tina introduced me to them as her daughter, so they were hands off right away, and they were real polite to me and stayed off of me.

The sailors came in on ships, and she knew them. The other girls were known to them, but I was a stranger. I was real little and skinny as hell, but they right away talked to me, and they came back for me, so Tina made money. She said to me, "Listen, I have a bottle here, and it is apple juice. When someone wants you to have a drink with them, tell them you want drink to apple juice." I couldn't say, "I have wine" when I didn't. That was against the law. And whatever I would drink with them, she would charge them and give me the money. So that's the way I made my money. When Tina was there I sat with her, and they could sit by us, but I couldn't sit in a corner somewhere that they couldn't see me. I had to stand and talk.

It was just after the war that they started the café. Charles helped his wife. Money he knew, business he knew, and they did make a lot of money there. I don't know if he was put into a camp, but I have a feeling he was. The way he talked, well, when it came to the Germans, he was not a nice person. But they never, never asked me questions about my stepfather. I was surprised, because you know my stepfather was S.S., and that was not a nice sign over your head. So I thought nobody was going to help me. But they always said in my language, "Oh, poor thing, poor thing."

I thought, "Why am I a poor thing?"

They thought I suffered so much for a little girl, I guess. That's what they told me.

Charles was always on the bouncy, happy side. We didn't know, but he always filled up the little ones with gin. Until Tina found out. She did one time. Oh, she was pissed. I thought she was going to kill him.

Charles talked like a firestorm. Oh, if you think I'm bad, he was worse. He could go on and on about the Germans, and the Americans, and the storms, there was always something. But you had to have a personality like that to run a café. He was really comfortable to me. In the morning I came down, I took care of the glasses, and the bucket of water. Charles did the floors, and we worked together while Tina slept. But he smoked horrible. Oh my God, when the Americans came in with all the cigarettes, his fingers were brown. He looked good for his smoking habits. I was worried about that, too, because he smoked those Players from England. It was like a Virginia tobacco, and they were awful.

They were very simple people. They were never dressed to go. Charles owned a little Volvo or something from Sweden, and once in awhile Tina asked him to drive along into town or outside in Antwerp. But she couldn't do much because she was so heavy. They lived upstairs in a nice apartment. On Sunday she closed everything up. She wanted to be alone and quiet, and then they sat there and listened to the radio. She liked books, too. She spoke four languages, German, and French, and she spoke my language, too. We had a funny dialect, and sometimes we laughed about it. The way we said things was real funky. His accent was different from hers.

They were happy with me, and they did everything for me, but I never knew anything about their side. She and her sister never got together. Funny. I never saw families there. Well, they lived funny there, believe me.

I asked her one time about the number tattoo, "Tina, what is that?"

"Oh, that was," her first husband was in the French Legion, and he sold her in Casablanca in a brothel. She said the guys paid for them, but they didn't get the money. Well, I don't know how she came out of there; she never told me that. That's where she got the number. That's what she said, but I cannot believe that. It was a concentration camp number, but she didn't want to tell me that, I think. The way she looked, she was a little bit older than him. But I don't know what she went through.

Charles liked soccer. That was the main sport, but Tina didn't let him go anywhere to watch the tournaments. Most of the time he sneaked to the store on the corner. He said, "Oh, Tina. I'll be right back. I'm going to the store to get this and this and this."

She said, "Okay." Then an hour later she said, "Where's Charles?"

I said, "He went to the store."

She said, "Go and get him!"

I thought, "Oh my God," you know. I said, "Okay!" So I went and when I came in there he sat listening to the dumb game on the radio. Well, in those times everything was on the radio, and he just goes there and lifts them. I told him, "You better get a mint or something. Oh God, if she knew."

So he said, "Okay."

In Belgium we got them Russian fish eggs, Caviar, and he took one spoon of that and he put it in his mouth, and then he chopped herring and then he ate it. Then by the time he got home and went in to her all she could smell was fish and onions.

I said, "Oh, I don't want to hear this."

"Oh no!" he said, "You stay here by me!"

I said, "Okay."

She came in, "What did you do down on the corner?"

"Oh," he said, "Listened to the soccer game on the radio and we talked."

"Let me smell your breath," she said.

"Oh, okay! I took two. Not much. Just two."

So she smelled his breath. "Oh, it stinks like fish."

Then he looked at me, and I had to go to the pot laughing my head off. But he didn't do anything else, you know. He worked hard, so he deserved that.

Most of the time on my time off, I went out with Tina, and we went next door and they did my hair, or I got a massage on my face. Sometimes we talked, and she wanted to know things from me. Then she would cry. She said, "I always wish I had a daughter."

I thought, "Well, you can adopt me." They were rich enough to do that. "I'm here by you," I said, "Whatever you want, I'll do for you, because you are so nice to take me in."

Then she said, "No, I don't want anything. You are just perfect."

CHAPTER TWENTY-SEVEN

WE'RE NOT TALKING ABOUT THAT

AS SOON AS THE SAILORS GOT OFF THE SHIP, THEY CAME IN SING-ing like crazy. They talked about the ocean, they talked about their wives, the food, the money. The weather gets cold, so most of the time in the winter they signed onto a ship for six months, and then the rest of the year they stayed home and did the farm. They told stories about the war, their kids, they brought some pictures, or they sat there and played some guitars.

It was 1948. The war was just over, remember that, and there was still a lot going on. Almost everyone went through the same situation, so we didn't talk about it. Life was too sad.

I don't know why, I can pick the Germans out, I can pick the Scandinavians out, I can pick the Jews out. Sweden had that beautiful blond hair and light skin. Norwegians are the same, except on the darker side. Denmark, you can see the Germans in them. It had to do with their nature. Germans are real stubborn. When you go to Bulgaria, the people are more lenient, and softer, and smoother, and not rough like Walloon and Hungary.

The songs are like that too. When you hear their songs, you will
pick it out. Italians have more love songs and quiet songs. The
other side is more pounding on the counter with drinks. I liked
the Irish men, too. They came in and were singing. Some of
them were soft spoken, some of them were tough and they stood
on the chairs singing songs about drinking. I think you have
that in any country. German ships came in, so we had Germans
coming in. They had beautiful songs for Germany, too. France I
didn't like so much. A Frenchman is more about himself. I liked
the Swedish. They were soft and mild, but they were the ones
that caused trouble.

Most of the time Norway and Denmark was okay, but when
the Swedes came in, oh, then you had fights. See, Denmark and
Norway was in the war with Germany. Sweden was neutral.
They went after each other like crazy and fought, and they're
tough. The police department was right across the street, so
when something happened, we had a bell, and the cops rushed
over and took the café over. Meanwhile I went to the pot, and I
closed the door, and I peed for a long time. I was scared, because
the guys were crazy. Sometimes they did break glasses, but then
they paid for them, and we were insured for that. Tina stood up
and talked to them, and said, "Listen, we are in Antwerp. We are
not in Norway or Sweden or Denmark. We're here in my house,"
she said. "And we're not talking about that. When you're nice
and sit down, I give you a drink for free." And they sat down
instantly. The fight was over.

Politics was a dangerous situation to talk about, so we never
did. The Cold War was a different story because it was too far
away to affect us. The Cold War was mostly in countries close to
the Russian zone. We knew what was happening, but we never
did talk about it, ever.

We had a big jukebox, and in the jukebox we had music from
every country. The sailors put the jukebox on, danced, and sang.

They spoke their own language. I learned to speak Dutch, and I already had German and France in my mind, so then I had to go over to Scandinavian. At first I could only serve them and say, "Thank you" or "Good day" to them in Scandinavian. Tina taught me that in the daytime when we had time. So little bit by little bit I learned it. Then I was much younger, so I picked things up easier.

We had a mirror behind the bar, so the minute somebody moved, I saw instantly what they did. Even when I had my back to the bar, I could see who was coming. They drank gin there. We weren't licensed to have hard liquor like gin or cognac. But they brought their own liquor in their back pocket so Tina couldn't see, and it was like gin or something. The first time I smelled it I thought I was going to die. But they did. They drank it. Some people loved it.

The beer in the café was tough. They had one dark, one light, and one medium. The sailors were on the ocean for months and they couldn't drink, and we knew that. The first time they came in from a long voyage, boy, you better give them a lot of water, because two beers and they were gone. When they were drinking too much and I saw they were overboard, I couldn't serve them no more. That was it. I had a bell, and I called, and the police walked in friendly, and then he sat down and talked to the guy, and then took him to the boat. Most of them were happy drunks. But when they were overboard they just fell on the floor and slept and they wouldn't move. We could do anything to them, and they wouldn't wake up. But Charlie was there on the corner with his taxi, so we called him, and he'd put him in the car and took the guy to the ship.

I liked one Scotch, Christmas and New Year. That's the only thing I had. I could drink wine, but I didn't. When they said, "Mona Lisa, you want to drink with us?"

I said, "Yeah!" I got paid for this. They spent money like crazy.

Tina said to me in my language, "You better get the juice, and hold onto the glass. Don't let them taste it." Because when they saw that was false, they would not pay for it. I told you before, that was against the law. The real beer cost maybe $10 and I drank a $2 Jewish wine, there was no alcohol in it, and they'd pay the full price for what I drank. It was not right to do that, but that's the way they did it. I didn't care. I made money. Five bucks was five bucks.

Some people who couldn't hold it in, they attacked the girls. Then out they went. We had a bouncer. Oh, he was a big guy, you know, a wrestler. He worked on the outside, walking from bar to bar, and he took care of the street and watched everything that went on.

It was fun, but I wouldn't do that again in my whole life. I was happy to get out of there. It was a job. I'd rather clean and cook. Stupid but true.

CHAPTER TWENTY-EIGHT

THAT IS NOT MY LIFE

THEY KNEW MY NAME, BUT THEY ALWAYS CALLED ME MONA Lisa. I don't know why they did that. They said, "Hi, Mona Lisa, we're back."

One regular customer of the café was a big huge Danish guy, a captain from one of the boats. He was gone for a long time. I thought he died. One day I came in, and there he was. "Hey! Mona Lisa!" He said, "Oh, I got some troubles, and we had to fix it, and as soon as it was fixed, I jumped on the boat and came back." And then he said he got a tattoo. Was a snake. He took his pants off, the whole café was full of people, and he said, "Look!"

I said, "Oh my goodness!" He got a snake all the way around. Everybody in the café turned blue. Oh God, when I think about that guy, he was something else. But they were big huge tough guys, oh shoot. They always brought me some gifts, souvenirs, clothes sometimes. They brought me shawls, scarves, beautiful bracelets, roses. I was scared because a lot of guys came to Tina off the boat, and when they were on the ocean for three months and they saw a woman, oh, they were pretty wild. And I was not a wild person. I told Tina, "I cannot handle them."

She said, "But they are nice."

"But I have still too much memories from my stepfather." I would've killed them if they touched me.

Inspector Beck understood that. I said to him, "I don't know. The guys want to kiss me, and I slap them." I said, "I'm not good to stay there, because I can't handle that."

"Well," he said to me, "You don't have to accept that." So he taught me. He said, "When they touch, tell them to be nice and stay away from you." And I did, because I didn't like that fluffy poop. I'm still like that.

Tina got me a wedding ring, and I put it on. Then I told them, "I'm married. My husband is on the ocean." Then they don't mess around with me. It was a lie, but I had to lie, because I didn't want those big guys grabbing my tutu.

One ship that came in were Irish guys, and one was singing to me. I thought the Irish songs was so pretty. They spoke in English, but the other girls there always told me what they said. But I understood the singing. It was still dangerous on the ocean, too, by the way. When the ship went back to sea it struck a mine, and everybody was killed. And for a long time every time I heard that song I would cry a river.

When I was there, there was a strike on the boats. So all the police were all by us in the street and they always came in for the coffee. The normal police wore black and white and had a little hat on. They came in your house like a friend. The state troopers wore blue and red, a belt across their chest, a red stripe on the side, and gloves, with a big hat on like a can on their head and they came only when there was riots, fire, and they patrolled the highways.

We had union strikes sometimes with the dock workers, for the benefits, or they were not getting paid enough. Oh, they had a lot of fights in the streets. When that happened we closed the restaurant. They hit each other, and then the cops came in. The strikes went on two or three weeks. But we had to be careful. There were riots because of the strikes. A whole bunch of guys would be going around looking for someone. We would call the cops and tell them what was going on, and then they followed them and said, "Hey, guys, come here. We have to talk to you. Talk it off, because the strike is over, and we not going to fight. Tell us what happened."

The first of the month all the police had their checks, and they came in and they would drink a beer. The police I could serve. None of them would hurt me. They put the jukebox on, and they said once in a while, "Rach, can I dance with you?"

I said, "Don't touch me."

"I promise not to," they said, and so I would dance with the cops.

Then they bought one rounder for everybody, you know. They said, "Charles, you, too!" So he lifted them, my God. Then it was okay with Tina. She watched him sitting there. Then after the cops were gone, he ate something and lay on the floor there in the kitchen for a long time. He was out. Boy, he was so happy when the first of the month came.

One policeman was crazy for me, and I always said, "I'm too young, I'm too young." So he always put on that song, "Too young." We would talk and talk and he would stay there for days and nights and watch the harbor. I'm not always looking when people came in, and he came in and followed me wherever I went, and he always put on the same old record, Dean Martin, "My Heart Cries for You."

Tina called me over to the kitchen and said, "Watch that uniform deal there. Uhn uh." She said, "You can talk, but I'm going to watch you."

So the policeman always came back and he brought me this and he brought me that. But he was married, and I said, "I don't know. Because you're married, you stay away from me."

"Okay." He said, "But I can come in any time I want to."

I said, "That's true. But don't buy me nothing. I don't want to accept it."

"Oh, okay." So I had to watch them. They were sneaky sons of a guns.

The other girls went out with the guys, but that was their problem, not me. They had their own apartments and they paid for it. They were older, too, twenty-four, twenty-five. They could do what they want. I couldn't. I listened to the rules.

Sonia had a little apartment there, and she was married to an American. She was constantly drinking and drunk. She was a beautiful woman, by the way. She had beautiful diamonds from her husband, a ring all the way around with diamonds. She never took it off, so no one could steal it. Her husband was on the ocean, but then he wrote her off saying he would stay in America. So she started drinking. They would find her here, find her there on the street. So finally we brought her in one night when she was laying there in the gutter. We took her in and put her in the kitchen. She was covered with waste and shit. We cleaned her up, and we put her to sleep on the couch. She was frozen half to death, so we wrapped her in a blanket and covered her up. Then one of the policemen came over and took her. He talked to her and then they took her to an institution. I didn't know that then, but that's what they did. She had been drinking gin and she was far gone. She couldn't keep her waste in. I learned from that. I thought, "That is not my life."

CHAPTER TWENTY-NINE

YOU ARE AND WILL BE HER CHILD

A GOOD FRIEND OF THE KUDLERS, AN OLD MAN FROM GHENT, came from the sea in a boat, and he stayed there in a little upstairs attic room. Tina called him "Father." He might be her father. She never said. He was tiny, real funny, and friendly. Whenever he came in, he hugged everybody. Well, I was not used to that. Nobody in my family hugged. But the guys were so happy to be home they kissed anything. Father started drinking until he fell on the floor. Then they picked him up and carried him upstairs.

People from Ghent stuck together all the time. He always came in and he said, "Hey, Kleine!" (He called me "little girl" in my language.) "I have money for you!" and he gave me some money to buy some clothes or something. He was so cute. I know, I had a good life with all the old people. I was raised by old people. I trusted them better.

Tina always said, "Come on, Papa. Give me your money." He would give everything up, and then she took his money and she put it in a little safe for him, so if something happened, he had money. Otherwise he would drink it all or give it away.

When we sat sometimes talking to the captains, the guys from the boat brought cameras and took pictures with the girls. Before they left for sea, Father got a picture with me.

I think when Father was on the ship, sometimes they went to Spain or India or Pakistan or whatever they did, and they couldn't get off the boat because it was dangerous there. So they sat and played cards or something. Then I bet Father showed around that picture of me.

When the boat returned, the old man came in, and he brought a whole bunch of friends over, and they drank and they talked, and that is where I met Nicolas Van Gyter.

Nicolas sat there when we were drinking and he watched me and we started talking about Ghent, about this, about that, and he thought it was horrible what happened to me. Later when they closed the café, Nicolas stayed there. There were three floors of apartments. That's where he lived. In the morning I came down and he made me breakfast. Nobody ever did that before, and I thought to myself, "Am I awake or something?" Most of the time I always ate alone. But we ate together, like I never did. He liked to eat. He loved good food.

Nicolas was tiny, short and chubby, real nice hands. He was maybe thirty-five or something, but he looked young for his age. His parents lived on the coast. He went to college, studied with the Maconist to be a radio operator, and his life was the boat. Most of the time we talked about my life. It was hard for me to go over it. But we didn't talk too much about him. Why, I don't know. I was not interested in him. I was awful.

He did tell me that during the war they were close to the English border at night when the ship was torpedoed. Most of the time the tankers went out to the oil company in Bombay for three months, six months, or the freighters brought food or furniture.

Not everybody survived, he said. They had a jacket, and on the jacket was two beacons, so the rescue crews could see them struggling in the water. English planes flew over and saw them in the water, and the English ships picked them up, I guess.

Tina told Nicolas about my parents, and Nicolas couldn't believe what happened to me. Then he asked Tina, "Can I go and see her parents? I want to see them."

Tina said, "Yeah."

I was reluctant to go back, but on a weekend when the café was closed, Nicolas rented a car and we drove to Ghent.

I came in with Nicolas, and my mother said to me, "Oh, fine to see you."

The kids were not there. I have no idea where they were. Maybe working. Geoff sat in the corner with the hat pulled over his glasses, and he looked like he was reading. He was scared of me after I clobbered him the one time. My mother said, "Oh, who's this?"

I said, "A good friend of mine. We wanted to go to Ghent, and we wanted to see some places, so that's why we came here." We didn't want to stay there.

My mother said, "Oh." So Nicolas talked to her, you know.

She still had no idea where I was working. We didn't talk about that. Well, the family always thought because I worked in a restaurant that I was a prostitute. I said, "No. If I were a prostitute, it would be up to me to sleep with the guy I wanted, not with the guy that wanted me." I told my mother, "So get that out of your damn mind."

Then Nicolas saw a picture of Hitler hanging on the wall, so he had to get out of there. He said, "I'm going to slaughter that guy." After that, we left.

Before we took off my Uncle Michiel called me and told me, "Don't even think about that guy. He's too old for you. He could be your father."

I said, "I know."

So in the meantime, we already had troubles from Hitler hanging there. We drove back, and then Nicolas looked at me and he said, "I hate those suckers."

"Then you have to hate me, too," I said, "Because I belong to the mother."

"No, it's not your fault. She was old enough to know what Hitler was. Geoff is an asshole because he is too lazy to work."

When I returned to Antwerp Tina said, "I have something for you. But I want you to come up to my room and open it."

I said, "Okay," and I opened it, and it was a letter from my stepfather.

Rachel,

Pressured by your mother, I am writing you this letter. She asks you why you do not want to come back home, and she said she really did not expect this behavior from you. Now that you are no longer a child, she expected more respect and consideration and wonders if it is because of your youngest brother, whom you have not been willing to see, or because the other children, whom you do not have to bother with and who won't give you problems. Maybe it's because of me. Here too you do not have to worry, because I agreed that you should come back home.

You can do what you need to do with your mother to arrange a place to sleep and stay and the necessary payments to cover the expenses for staying with us. You have to take care of your own wardrobe, and whatever job or work you want to do, which does not concern me. You will not recognize me anymore, for I have changed so much that I do not need anybody to take care of my household.

So, you see, if you have any respect for your mother you would give her that satisfaction by coming back home to live with her because now she knows that I have nothing against you. She would talk about you all day long. Everything will be forgotten by your mother as well as by me because we are tired of talking about the same thing all the time. She has very little to do with the family anymore because she always defended you from their shortsighted views or opinions.

And now at your age she can explain to you what she had to endure before she met me so that you will understand so you will be on her side and not on the opposite side of the family. What your mother would do should you refuse to come back home I do not know and I do not want to interfere, but one thing you should know is that your mother does not want to criticize you but longs for you to be with her, and mothers are like that. Now, to prevent problems should you decide to come back home, let us know so that we can organize everything, and your mother hopes to hear from you.

Do not forget everything is forgotten about what happened earlier with me and your mother. If you would like to come home you can enjoy happy days with your mother because you are and will be her child, and then her wish she desired will be fulfilled. You know like I do that this is my only wish, and that is to make her happy, and that is the reason I wrote this letter. Bye.

Best greetings,
Mr. & Mrs. Geoff Voorst Helene
Oudburg 45, Ghent.
6/4/1950

I said, "Tina, what the hell is he talking about 'forgive what you did?'" I didn't do shit to her, you know. I thought, "That's bull." But he knew that I was twenty-one, so I made more money. He wanted me back there by my mother to make money, I guess.

Betty was another café owner on the corner. Her husband was a captain on what they called the Holland-America Line, from New York to Belgium. He was black, by the way. Betty was a gypsy, and her parents were killed when the Germans took over the country. Her and her sister survived. She opened that restaurant, and her sister worked with her there. I didn't know them that long. We were friends and her sister and I went out sometimes. A few months later, her sister got sick and died. At that time we didn't know what it really was. I have a feeling it was cancer, but nobody in those times talked about cancer.

Betty came out and talked to me. She said, "There was a couple here last night, and they asked for you. They are from Ghent, and we said we don't know where you are."

I told her, "No. I don't want nobody from my family to know where I am."

CHAPTER THIRTY

I HATE PEOPLE LYING TO ME

IN THE BEGINNING WHEN WE MET, NICOLAS VAN GYTER AND I got a big problem. He was more cynical about individual human nature and not that forgiving to people. I was always more lenient, because I thought most of the time it was not the little people's fault for their misery, but the big shots. They were the ones that made the rules, and they were the ones that wanted to make us stupid, and it was the same thing in the Congo, I told him. At that time a revolution was going on in the Congo, and people were being killed like crazy. To settle the argument, Nicolas wanted me to go with him to the Congo and see how bad it was. It was just about three weeks there and three weeks back. I didn't really want to go. I was scared, and I didn't like boats at all.

I asked Inspector Beck, and he really didn't like it, but that's what Nicolas wanted, so finally I relented and we went. I had to get a paper from the state saying I could do this, I couldn't do that. I wouldn't be able to get off the boat, because I didn't have the shots, and I didn't have a passport. It was a big metal Belgium passenger steamship that brought people like the nuns back. Oh, I was sick the whole time. I sat in a little hammock and I went "boom, boom, boom!" I thought I was going to jump overboard or something. I saw nothing but the harbor; desert, desert, and desert, sand, sand, sand. There was nothing there. But I didn't go all the way to the Congo. We were only a few days from Antwerp, and they stopped the boat, and I decided to come back on the train.

After the war when all of the Americans finally left, Tina said, "I'm tired now." She ran the café for so long. I was then twenty-one, I had my passport, so I thought, "When you go, I go." I was already looking around for an apartment.

The Kudlers bought a little villa somewhere outside of the town, and Tina asked Nicolas if he wanted to take over the café. So Nicolas came back off the boat and signed the papers. The contract was for six months and he put a down payment on it. Then he wanted to take the last boat to pay all this off.

Nicolas said to me, "You want to help me? I'll keep you here, you can keep your room upstairs, and you take care of the café while I'm on the ocean, and I pay for everything." So whatever I made in the café when he was gone, I got to keep for myself. I was not a café woman, but I could handle it, you know. So I said, "That's a deal." And he paid the rent for the café. I didn't have a big salary; they paid me with rocks and stones in Europe. It was little what you got. But Nicolas wanted to stay with me for good.

So we took over the café from the Kudlers. I did the work behind the bar, and Nicolas went to sea. I never saw the Kudlers again. Well, I was busy with my own troubles. After the Kudlers left, we didn't have that much Americans no more. I got a lot of people coming back. A lot of people didn't come back, but I was comfortable there with whatever I got. I had still all the Scandinavian people coming in, Norwegian, Sweden, and Denmark. I did my best to make money, but that was it.

By the time I took over, I was pretty comfortable, because I knew the police department was there. They said, "Rachel, you have a bell. Ring the bell whenever trouble comes." Father, and all the people I knew, and the Maritime Company, it was right across the street, and they all knew me. At 12 o'clock I closed the door, and then it was over, you know.

Two girls did the work and served and everything else. The other girl was new to the job, but she didn't stay long. Whatever we sold, I had to pin the receipts, and on the weekends Inspector Beck came and he helped me to do all the paperwork, paying the salaries, and so.

Nicolas used me more for a convenience for him. I thought, "Well, he needs help, so I can help him out till he comes back." That's what I thought. I had no vision of the future. In my mind, I never thought I'd ever get married. No kids, either. Absolutely not. But slowly it developed after they left the café with us.

I didn't love. I'm still confused about that. People say, "I love that person so much I'm going to kill myself." I never got that. I can please, you know. I can help people, and we can help each other. When it came to sleeping, then I locked the door. I said, "No, no, no, that's as far as we go." First of all, I was not prepared for that. Second, I didn't want kids, and third, I was scared from diseases. Charles told me and Inspector Beck told me, "So soon you go to bed with the guy, he knocks you off your feet." And I always remembered that. I always was scared to do that. But I chose Nicolas because he was older, he was wiser, and he was more like a father than a lover. I was young. I suppose I thought I was free from all the misery.

Nicolas was a nice person, and he was clean. He was a really good-looking guy, and he was not playing, that's what I thought. Financially he was much, much better than me. He was a radio operator, his salary was high, and he was pretty good to me, so I thought that was what I needed. Somebody that I could trust. But it didn't work out that way.

The day Nicolas was coming, I was working the café, and I was going to pick him up around two o'clock. She was a tiny chubby blonde, blue eyes, with a dialect. She spoke English, and I couldn't understand. I looked from the kitchen, and she sat in the corner. One of the girls said to me, "There's a lady, and she wants to talk to you. Is Mrs. Van Gyter."

I thought, "Mrs. Van Gyter? That's funny. Who can she be?" I thought, "His brother's wife," not knowing.

Then the girl came back and said, "Yeah, she wants to talk to Mr. Van Gyter over the son, because Mr. Van Gyter don't pay for the kid."

I thought, "That has to be him." Then I got the picture, and I thought, "Something is wrong." I didn't talk to her. It was his business, not mine. So I said to the girl, "Do you mind taking over, because I think I'm going to go upstairs. I'm going to wait for Mr. Van Gyter there. Tell him when he comes in to come up."

She said, "Okay."

Nicolas came back into port. This time I wasn't there to pick him up, so he took a taxi. He came in, he saw Mrs. Van Gyter, and he knew, "Uh oh, something's wrong here." When Nicolas came upstairs to my room and came through the door, I had a beautiful big brass candlestick. I picked it up and hit him over the head, "Poot!"

Then he held his head, and he said, "What did you do that for?"

I said, "Because you lied to me, and that is your punishment."

He said, "No, I don't. I just keep it away from you because I knew you'd dump me."

I said, "You're right. Now you're dumped right there," and I said, "You better get rid of her, or I'll get the other candle and smack her over the head." Stupid, but I was mad. I couldn't handle that people lied to me. Okay, they had been separated, because she had been hitting around or something. He had a kid, too, by that woman. That's not right to do that to that kid. I hate people lying to me.

Nicolas said, "Okay, I'll take care of it," and he left, and I never heard of her again. Maybe he threw her in the ocean, I don't know. He told me he had met her when she was a nurse in the hospital in England.

He said, "Well, she crawled with me in bed."

I said, "Well, you was not that sick then, when you could make a baby."

He said, "I'm separated anyway, so what's the difference?"

I said, "A lot. You lied to me, and I don't trust you no more." That was it for me. So I said, "You can have your bar, and I'm leaving."

He said, "No, you can't. You and me signed a contract."

So I had to wait.

Before he went to the ocean, he said to me, "Okay, then let us be friends. I'm going to take a trip for three months and think it over."

I said, "There's nothing to think over."

But, see, for me it was easy to walk away. I didn't want that attachment. When the time comes, you're going to see the right story, and you see how the thing is.

CHAPTER THIRTY-ONE

YOU KNOW THE FAMILY

I ASKED INSPECTOR BECK, "WHAT SHALL I DO ABOUT THIS LET-ter from Geoff?"

Inspector Beck said, "Don't answer it."

A few months later my mother had another baby. I didn't notice she was pregnant the last time I saw her. Well, she was always heavy duty. By then I got my passport and on that passport it said where I lived. So one of my cousins called the police department, and they gave her my address and phone number.

My aunt Jenny called. Erwin was the godfather for the baby, and Jenny told me my mother wanted me to be a godmother. My mother still didn't know where I was. I never talked to her because of Geoff. I was still hateful then, and I couldn't stand him.

You know what I don't understand? She never went to church, she hated the church, she was not even married with Geoff, but she still baptized all the kids. Why she wanted me for the god-mother, I don't know. I have a feeling she wanted to see me. In my mind, I really didn't want to go. But I thought, "Well, maybe

I'll see her." So I did it for my mother, and I did it for the baby. The baby is always innocent.

The baptism was in Ghent. My mother held the baby by a big water fountain, and then they put water over his head and said, "bless this, bless this, and bless this." Erwin and I held the baby, too, and they blessed it. I carried a candle in my hand; was a whole ceremony. Not too many people were there. My mother and the kids, Sarah, Antoine, and Simon.

After the ceremony, I talked to Erwin. I was closer to Erwin. Then Erwin told me, "Did you know that Moo died?" Moo was my grandmother.

I said, "No, nobody told me."

He said, "No, nobody wanted to, because everybody says you was a whore anyway."

I said, "Well, I go from bastard to whore. What's next?"

My uncle said, "You know the family."

I said, "Yes, I do." And I was so sad, because my life was not like that at all.

Erwin told me the whole story, that when he found my grandmother, she had to be already a day or two dead, and nobody knew.

The last time I saw my grandmother before I left for Antwerp it was a trauma, because she always wanted to keep me, and I couldn't stand it. So after that I never went to see her again. That bothered me, too, because she raised me. I thought in my mind there was going to be a curse on my life because she did so much for me, and I didn't do nothing to help her when she needed somebody.

After the baptism ceremony, I met my other uncles and had a coffee and a cake or something. It's funny, they all changed in different ways, you know.

After the furniture incident, Edmond never had any more problems about working for the Germans. I told you that the family from my Aunt Sarah helped him out of that mess. So after the war Edmond started his own business again as a painter and remodeler. He made good money, too. A lot of houses were destroyed by bombs, so there was a lot of work for him. He hired an assistant, because he couldn't do all what he did before the war. That was better for him, you know. They were not rich, rich, but they were comfortable, and they only had one daughter. Edmond was so-so with his brothers. Most of the time he and my Aunt Sarah stayed in their house, they cooked, they had their books and their music on all the time. They were not going-out persons like we are here.

Their daughter Nathalie grew up a little bit medium in size and worked in the laundry with her mother. The Laundromat in Ghent was a big huge company. They put the clothes through a machine, folded and ironed them for you, and delivered them back to your home. Like me, Nathalie's education was cut short by the war. That she went back to get an education, I have no idea. I don't think so. But she's still alive, and we're still good friends.

Michiel didn't have problems after the war, either. Everything was taken care of in Germany. The benefits were good. My Aunt Amandine got problems with her teeth, so they fixed her teeth in Germany, and they saved all their money. After they returned from Germany, Michiel went back to the weaving mill making satin for blouses. He had a boy after Sandrine. They took the money they had saved in Germany, and they bought a little house next door to his mother-in-law. They raised their kids there, and they lived in that house until they died. Michiel changed a lot after his experiences in Germany. He was more mellow, and my Aunt Amandine, too. But his kids grew up in that little house and they were happy.

I don't think Jenny or Erwin worked after the war. But I'm not sure, because I was not there. Jenny was sick. She could hardly walk she was so heavy. They didn't do that good financially, but they did do. They lived in the same place until they died, both of them. She was lazy and didn't do nothing, and she didn't want nothing to do with the church, and I don't know. My Aunt Jenny was eating a piece of pie, that's what they told me. She loved to eat, and my cousin was in the kitchen. When she came back my aunt lay on the table, like she fell asleep or something. So, she looked, and she had died with the pie in her mouth. It was a massive heart attack, I guess.

In the war Fredric worked in a mill grinding wheat, and from that wheat they made bread. Well, these machines created a lot of dust, the factories were not clean in those times, and they had no protective material. That damaged his lungs, and he later got an operation, and lost his throat. So they put a hole in his larynx, and from then on he had to talk with a machine. In that time, Europe was not blessed with all the doctors like here. We don't know here how blessed we are. My Aunt Marie had an aunt and an uncle with a lot of money, and they never married, so the money stayed in the family and went to all the kids, you know. Fredric was a quiet man, but he was always pissed off at me.

Florence helped her mother crocheting and knitting. Oh, they were fantastic. Florence made a beautiful painting for me in needlepoint. We were never that close, though, and there was always that division between us, because I was still the "Snow White" girl. When Florence got out on her own, then it changed, because her husband was not that well-to-do, and he was sick, so then she moved back in with her parents. I don't think she ever stood on her own feet. She always went back to her parents.

I always thought growing up, "Oh, they love me, they love me!" But when I came back from Antwerp I was wiser, I was somewhat smarter, and I knew the love they had given to me before and during the war was only for using me to clean the house or to get the food. So I said, "Okay, that is what the case is all about." I learned more about people.

The funny part was, they always talked about how bad I was. Well, Morgane, Florence's sister, was born in the war, but she was a whole different ballgame. Oh my goodness, she was not like Florence at all. She came out like, "Hey, I'm Mrs. So-and-So," she loved expensive stuff, and she really struck them hard with the money, you know. She dressed to kill, and she wouldn't have anything but the best. And I was so happy to hear that. I said, "Thank you, Lord." They always blamed me, now they had their own problems. Morgane's marriage was a big thing, but then it didn't work out. Her husband later left her and moved in with a guy. So that was not a nice picture for the family, either. But that was okay with me. They had to learn the hard way.

Everybody knew why I left. But some of them still thought I worked in the red light district. They thought, "What else can she do?" I had no education, remember that. That don't mean I had to be a whore. I don't believe that either. I couldn't write, no. But I could talk.

Somewhere I think Michiel heard that I was working in the Antwerp red light district. He sent people out to check on me, because he was concerned for me. I always think now, that's who that couple was who asked Betty about me, but I never found out for certain. Michiel was pissed off at my mother. He blamed my mother for that. He said, "You pushed her there."

My mother and him had a big fight. My mother said, "I don't know, I don't know, I don't know." You know, my mother never knew anything. But I still never told him where I was.

Sofie always remained in the hospital. She never came out, and she never did improve. She was dangerous, too. You could just be sitting there, and for no reason she would come over and smack you. That's what happened in the institution, too. I did see her again years and years later. A long time she had been in there, and I thought, "Wow, she's not going to remember me." But she did, and she was really happy to see me. But she never changed, and she died in the institution. But of all my aunts and uncles, she lived the longest, and she died only recently. Sofie had two sons, and one that didn't talk to the family. He was raised in an orphanage, you know, so he had a different attitude. He wanted nothing to do with the family, I guess.

The family stood away from my mother for a long time. Except later when my uncle was going up for his anniversary, or when somebody died, then they would invite my mother over and let her be with her family, you know. But most of the time they never contacted her. They loved my mother, but they didn't like Geoff. My uncles said later, "We knew that you left because of him." But I kept my mouth shut. I had siblings, Geoff was their father, and I didn't want to hurt them. And the kids never talked about that, either.

After that last visit with my family, I took off again, because I had to get back for my business. I caught the last bus to Antwerp at ten o'clock.

CHAPTER THIRTY-TWO

NOBODY KNOWS BUT ME

ON MY WAY BACK THE BIG STORM CAME, AND A DYKE IN HOL-
land broke. The main area of Europe is below sea level, and it is
surrounded by dykes. During the storm, the dyke in Holland just
gave out, and certain areas, Netherlands, England, France, Denmark, and Belgium were flooded. They tried to stop it. They had
the military and volunteers there with sandbags. But I believe
something like 2,000 people died that night.

We drove back to Antwerp in the rain and wind. We made
it to the station, and I went home with the taxi. That is when
the water started rising, slowly flooding the streets. I opened the
gate to the cellar where the barrels of tapped beer was kept. The
barrels were flying around, and I thought, "What the hell happened?" And then I saw the cellar was under water. Everything
was full of beer all over the place. So then I thought, "It's going to
be bad news here."

I went up and got my suitcase. We could see the ships from
where we were, and by then I saw the water coming in, and the
ships going backwards and forwards. I took all my clothes, I

didn't have much, and I took Nicolas's dumb shit, he was out on the ocean, and I got out of there. Then the café and the whole saboo went under water.

Antwerp was partially flooded. Not Ghent. I don't think so, but I was in Antwerp when that happened. That whole street was flooded. It was a mess there.

I was writing letters to Nicolas, who was out to sea, so he knew what happened. I told the company to telegraph that I would find an apartment and take his clothes with me. The letter took forever, eight days. Nicolas telegraphed me back and said, "Okay, I will pay the rent." And that's what he did. I was happy, because I didn't make that much money. So I took care of his stuff, and I brought it wherever I went.

It took awhile to fix the flooded ports. They put machines on it, and I don't know. That's why we left the restaurant.

Antwerp at that time had a lot of houses, but most of the time people lived together because after the war there were still lots of places that had to be cleaned up and rebuilt. There was a huge section where the boats came in, with a lot of offices and buildings where they loaded and unloaded cargo, the people worked and shoveled around, you know, and right next to that was the city itself. They had music stores, and a theater called the "Billiard Palace," where people performed, they had the streetcars and trolley busses; a lot of people still walked around and rode their bicycles.

I told a beautician I knew ran a boarding house that I had to get out and I was looking for a little room till I found a nice apartment. She said, "Well, you can stay with me."

I said, "Oh, okay."

So I looked, but the room was real tiny, all the way up at the top in the attic. I thought, "Well, let me take it for a month till Nicolas comes, then we can look together for an apartment." So I got all his things there, you know.

Maybe two nights I stayed there, and then in the middle of
the night Nicolas came in with the ship, and he came over to the
boarding house. We were eating and talking about what we were
going to do with the dumb restaurant, and there came the cops
knocking on the door. They came in, and they said, "We want to
talk to Nicolas Van Gyter."

I said, "Okay."

And then they saw me, and one of the cops knew me from my
café. He said, "Hey, Rach, what are you doing here?"

I said, "Well, Nicolas just came in with the ship. We had to
get out of the restaurant. So I rented this little place until I could
find something."

He said, "Did you know the guy was married? His wife is
chasing him." At that time there was a law that you could not
register in the same room unless you were Mrs. and Mr. Nicolas said that he was separated, but he had to pay for the kids or
something. I never had kids, so I didn't know about paying for
kids. But for some reason the wife wanted the police to catch
Nicolas with another woman. They knew the ship was in, so
they followed him.

But the police did trust me, because the police department
knew me. They were always in my restaurant. I didn't know
really what the case was all about. So I said, "What should I do?"
I was in my pajamas. I said, "I slept here."

He said, "Yeah, but nobody knows but me."

The cops said, "We'll take her away from here."

Then they helped me pack up my stuff and got me out of the
apartment. I don't know what really happened after that, and
Nicolas and I never went over it again.

CHAPTER THIRTY-THREE

WHAT THE HELL IS HE WHISTLING AT ME FOR?

AFTER THAT, THE POLICE HELPED ME, AND I TOOK MY THINGS and left. I still took Nicolas's clothes with me, because he didn't have an apartment.

The ship foreman that worked with Nicolas had a little house there with his wife, two daughters, and his father, an old man who was about ninety. The foreman came in with Nicolas all the time, and I knew the girls because they worked delivering telegrams. Nicolas asked them to help me, so they found a nice little apartment for me next door. I liked it, because it was close to the police department. I stayed in the apartment and Nicolas paid the rent. I didn't want to stay with Nicolas, so he stayed with the foreman in his house for two days, and then he made ready to go back to sea. Before he left, he brought me a bird, a little yellow canary.

One time I came out of the apartment and across the street was the police building. A guy across the street wolf-whistled. I looked at him, and he was a big tall boy, skinny, dark, and I thought he was a Hawaiian. I thought, "What the hell is he whistling at me for?" Because nobody whistled at me. I was not that pretty. Then he went into the police department.

After Nicolas left again, the restaurant was still flooded. I got a job with the foreman's daughters delivering telegrams. They were simple girls. They helped me with my telegrams, and we went together to work and off work. The telegrams came from the ship department. About one week I had training and that was it, then I followed a list from the office, and I already knew my route. One of the girls, she helped me with that.

Antwerp was split. One part was diamonds; one part was ships that came in from all over the world. All of the ships companies were at the harbor. The business people wrote to the ships when I came in and then they did business, buying merchandise, cargo, and the ship offices sent the telegrams to all the big companies listing all the ships that were coming in. I had one round in the morning, one in the afternoon, and one in the evening. I ran real fast and brought the telegrams to all the different offices in town. I was like a toothpick, and I knew all these offices out of my head, you know.

About that time, Inspector Beck came over to the house and asked me to help him out. He said there were two guys from Holland, and they were bringing black market gin into these pubs and selling this hard liquor. After the war, there was a lot of black market. Inspector Beck said, "Can you help us out with another girl?" He wanted us to go into the pub with them, talk to them, and get out of them everything about where they hung around and what they sold.

I said, "Okay." So I had to go to this dance hall where they wanted to sell the gin and entertain them with another girl, Maria. Maria was kind of a big blonde. I knew her from the Kudler's café. She was one of the girls helping out, and then later she got a better job in town.

We went into the dance hall, and there was a Hawaiian band playing. For the second time I saw this kid who whistled at me, and I remembered his face from the police department, and he was playing guitar. I thought, "Oh, that is that Hawaii guy." But I didn't think nothing about it at that moment, you know.

We were sitting there in this dance hall, and they came in, and then Maria looked at them, and she started talking to them like she knew them. They said, "Do you know her?"

Then Maria said, "I'm sorry, I got the wrong person."

And they said, "We are from Holland."

Maria said, "Oh, that's nice," and she started making conversation with them. Maria was different from me. She knew how to talk and how to entertain, because she went out more.

Finally they said, "Do you mind if we sit down with you?"

Maria said, "No." So then they ordered some drinks or whatever, and we danced with them. A policeman and a police woman came in later, but they were not in uniform, so you could not see that they were police. They were like man and wife, and they sat down at another table and talked, and they watched them. So I said, "Oh, we going to go to the toilet." So when we left, then the cops took over. They got them and their car. The car was full of black market gin.

Marcus, the guy that owned a café called the Oberbayhren, knew my mother. The Oberbayhren was a nice place, a German place, by the way. Marcus and my mother were in the same meeting one time. Marcus had a beard, and he was kind of blondish. He was in the war in Italy when the war was just beginning with the Russians. When he was there, I don't know what happened; I think he was in the front line. He was shot, and he lost his legs just above the knees. He was picked up, and they brought him to a hospital in Germany. Hitler went in to see the wounded, so Marcus met Hitler. Hitler listened to his story, and then he got prosthetic legs from Hitler, and Hitler became his godfather.

Marcus was very robust, because he relied on his arms and his upper torso to move around. He looked funny. I think he got his prosthetics right where his lower thighs were, and I don't remember ever seeing him walking on crutches, either. Marcus stood not firm on his legs, so when you touched him, he fell over.

So when he saw me he said, "Rach, I want you to help me in my store."

I said, "Why?"

"Well," he said, "You can make some good money."

I said, "Yeah, okay."

The Oberbayhren was a big place with a big dance floor. They had long benches, and long wooden tables, and sometimes when the German band played their "oomp pa pa" music, they would lock arms, lift up their beers and sing: "Hey, have a drink on me!" It was a rough place. Especially at that time. You couldn't breathe because of the smoke. People lined up to get in, you know. There were a lot of sailors there, Swiss, Norwegian, German, and French. The crowd in the pub were very familiar. They were real nice; it was almost an extended family.

So after delivering telegrams, I came home, took a shower, laid down for awhile, then I went into the Oberbayhren some time before six and set up all the tables. When they opened, the people came in, and it was raining and cold, so they had a hat on and a big coat and gloves and a shawl. Then they took all that off, and I put numbers on there, and then they went and danced and drank, and whatever. Sometimes they were drunk and forgot their stuff, and they went out in the street, they came back the next day and said, "Do you still have my coat and my hat and my gloves?"

I said, "You got your ticket?"

They said, "Yeah!"

"I'll get it." Then I got a big tip. When it came to a tip, boy, I was ready. Marcus got me a salary, plus I got tips from the people who brought the coats in. When a girl was not there, I jumped in for the girl, and I made more money. Most of the time I worked on Christmas day. I worked through all the holidays. But I did go to the church when I got off. I worked in the winter, because I made more money. More people had hats or coats or gloves and they went out all dressed up, their hats, to celebrate dancing and so.

The Oberbayhren had a six-piece German band, and we called it the "oomp pa" band, because they sang all the "oomp pa, oomp pa" music. There was an accordion player, a drummer, and then they had the tuba, the bass, and they wore little green hats with the feather, brown leather pants, with the beautiful edelweiss flowers on their chest, stockings to the knees, everything was green and brown, white shirts, short sleeves.

I knew Harry, the guitar player. When I ran the café with Nicolas, once in awhile he came over and played. He was a lone street musician then. He had a guitar and a harmonica, and he had a bucket there, and everybody put money in. Sailors that came in there off the boats, they were wild, and when they were drunk, they grabbed me and kissed me. Harry always stepped in and helped me. I didn't see him no more for a long time until I went to the Oberbayhren. There he was. He came over, and then he asked me what happened. Sometimes he brought me to my apartment so that I was not alone. But he had a wife and kids.

After an hour or so the German band stopped, took a break and ate a meal or something, and then a four-man Hawaiian band came up for an hour, the Royal Hawaiian Minstrels. They were all good-looking. The guitar player was the youngest of all of them. Someone was on the ukulele, steel guitar, and then there was a bass. The ukulele player's wife came up and danced the hula and the candle dance, they called it, where she danced with two candles on her hands. When they were done, then the German band went up again. And that kept up from eight till around six o'clock in the morning. It was a long time.

Marcus was quiet, but he was disciplined, and we followed his rules. He said to us, "You don't dance with nobody." And that means nobody. He said that customers couldn't dance with the personnel, and he was real strict about that.

One time the Hawaiian band hired a percussion player from Brussels. He said, "I'd like to enhance your music with my bongos."

The bandleader said, "Well, okay, we'll try you for one night."

So he played his bongos, and he knew how to play that thing. But he wouldn't back down for no rules, no regulations, and during a break he saw me there working. He said, "Lady, let's go dance." So he was dancing with me and nothing was said. But when it was over, Marcus went up to him, tapped on his shoulder and said, "You know the regulations here. You cannot dance with personnel, because you work here at this place."

He said, "Well, who are you to be telling me this?"

Marcus said, "I'm the boss. I own this thing."

"I don't care. I want to dance with who I want!"

Marcus said, "Leave her alone. Don't touch her, because I knock you off your feet."

He laughed, because the boss had no legs. "One push from me and you lay on the floor."

So Marcus said, "You try it," because Marcus was bigger and stuff.

Boom! They fought. He got thrown out. There, when two fight, the rest fights. Marcus fell on the floor and he hit his head on the side of a table and cut open his eye.

I don't know what happened after that because there was a whole bunch of shit going on, and the cops started coming in, so I split out through a side door.

CHAPTER THIRTY-FOUR

WHAT THE HELL AM I GOING TO DO WITH THAT KID?

MY GIRLFRIEND MARIA WORKED FOR AWHILE AT THE OBER-bayhren as a waitress. She asked for help, if she could stay with me for a little while. She had no place. I said, "Yeah, okay, you can stay in my room, but I have to do this and this and this, so I'm not always home, but I want you to keep it clean." I'm a clean woman.

She said, "Okay, just for sleeping." So sometimes she was there, sometimes she was not. The Oberbayhren was big, and Maria was in the back. Everybody had three or four tables to serve. Then mysteriously she disappeared on me. I didn't see her for a few weeks. So finally after a whole long time, she came in with a doctor from Switzerland, and she said, "Guess what, we're going to get married!" And she was so happy.

Then I found out she had been involved with a man from Brussels. He wanted her to help him working on cocaine or something. You know, some assholes don't take no for an answer, and he came after her. He took her out to dinner, dropped something in her drink, and she woke up in a brothel in Casablanca. She had been sold there. So this doctor from Switzerland had found her there and paid her out.

At that moment I was working, and she was sitting getting some wine or tea or whatever she was drinking with her husband. Her things were still there in the apartment, she was going to pick it up, and then she and her husband were going to leave for Switzerland. But before she left the Oberbayhren, I heard screaming and yelling, and I saw a commotion. I thought somebody hit somebody for dancing. And then I saw all the blood on the floor, and I thought, "Oh shoot, what happened here?" And then I knew, the guy from Brussels who sold her came in, and then he sliced her face open.

I was in shock. Her husband got a lot of ice right away and put it on her face. The boss called the ambulance, and she was taken away. We had to clean the floor; she was bleeding like crazy. I never saw a face popping up that fast.

Always when a break came at the Oberbayhren, I sat down and ate herring. I never ate much. I was eating my herring, and the guitar player from the Hawaiian band came next to me, and he said, "Do you mind that I sit down next to you?"

I said, "No." And I thought, "Why is he sitting next to me?" because the herring and the onions stunk. When I ate it, I went and cleaned my teeth right away.

He said his name was Lud. "Oh, you got a wedding ring. You're married."

"Yeah," I said, "I'm married." So I looked at him. He was real young. Eighteen.

He said, "Oh." But he didn't believe me. I could see it on his face. He thought, "Well, she's too young to be married, and if she's married, what would she be doing working here at night?" So he said, "What time are you done?"

I said, "When I am done."

"Oh, me too," said he. "Can we meet after that and have soup?"

I said, "Sure."

"I want to talk to you," he said.

I said, "Okay." But I thought to myself, "Why you want to talk to me?" You know, because I'm working, I'm old, I'm busy, I'm married, all these things in my mind.

He said, "Well, let's not make people suspicious about our relationship. So I'll go ahead and I'll see you there." We had to, otherwise we'd lose our jobs, because we were working at the same place and Marcus had a policy that the employees couldn't dance together, did not go together, and all that kind of stuff.

Harry, the accordion player in the German band, he was after me, but he had a wife and kids. He never let me go alone to the streetcar. He always said to me, "I'll bring you to the streetcar that I know nothing happens to you."

Then I was talking with Harry in the street and I looked up and saw Lud in the doorway. I thought, "Oh my God, I forgot all about that I was supposed to meet him." But I didn't want to tell Harry anything, because I knew he was German and Lud was dark, that don't work together. So there was the streetcar and I left, and Lud was stuck there alone, poor guy.

The next night Lud said, "I'm not going to wait for you anymore. I'm in the hotel. You come and see me."

So that's what I did. But we didn't talk long, because we had to work all night. I told him, "You know, I don't think this relationship will work, because I have a bad childhood."

After that, we went to work separately, so we were not seen together, and then from work we went to a restaurant or something. We didn't eat much in the afternoon, and we started working at nine o'clock at night. So most of the time we went with all the musicians, and had a cup of soup or something.

Lud told me he was originally from Indonesia, but they had relocated to Holland where he finished his schooling. He didn't want to stay in Holland, because of the racial tension there. He tried everything to split to another country. But then he was approached by a guy, like he landed out of Mars or something, and he said, "Do you play an instrument?"

Lud said, "Yeah, I play a little bit of guitar because I'm taking lessons."

He said, "Can you come over and see if you can play some songs with us and sing, because we're trying to form a group and go travel through Europe. Belgium, France, Germany." They were going to try and start in Belgium.

So Lud said, "Okay, I'll come up with something."

The leader had a reel-to-reel tape set up, and he had a couple of songs, and Lud picked something he knew. So they sang together, and sang close harmony, and Lud played the few chords he taught him how to play, and it sounded okay, according to the bandleader. So he said, "Would you like to come with me and travel?"

Lud said, "Okay," because he didn't like Holland anyway.

He said, "Ask your mom and dad and see what they think about it."

Lud asked his mom, "What do you think?"

Lud's mom said, "Well, it is your life. It is your future."

So Lud went back to the guy and said, "Okay."

They taught Lud their songs, and then they hopped on the train and they took the Amsterdam-to-Paris train to Belgium. The first stop was in Kortrijk and they got out of the train, and all their instruments, and Lud thought, "Now what?"

The bandleader said, "There's a little café. Let me go in there and talk to the guy." He went in and said, "Hey, I want to play for you for free, if it's okay, to draw customers for you."

The owner said, "What kind of music do you play?"

He said, "Hawaiian music."

The owner said, "Huh? What is that?" So he said, "Okay." They came in and set up everything, and then they started playing and singing. And sure enough customers were looking: "Where's that funny sound coming from? What's that all about?"

So after playing two or three times, the bandleader went to the owner and said, "Look, we're drawing a lot of customers here. You don't have to pay us, but do you mind if we collect?" The bandleader went around and asked for money from the crowd first. And then another one of the band members got to do that. Lud was eighteen. The other guys were in their thirties. So come the third time, the bandleader told Lud, "It is your turn now." Lud thought he was going to die, he was so embarrassed. But you know he just bit his tongue and did it. So after that they stopped, and the following day they went to another place and did the same thing all over again. And while they were doing that they talked to other people to set them up to play on a weekly basis. And that's how they came to be playing in Belgium.

Lud told me, "Belgium are different people from Holland. They are introverts. They're not as outgoing as the Dutch people." He said you could see in their body language what they thought about them with the dark skin. But they accepted that because Lud said, "We told them we came straight from Hawaii, and they believed us. Everybody swallowed it, so it was okay."

Lud told me the ukulele player reported to the police that he came from practice and he found his wife dead. And then they found out it was an abortion. She was not that big, so nobody knew she was pregnant. She wanted to stay with the band, because they were making money, and she looked into getting an abortion.

Abortions were all clandestine, in private, and in secret. Usually they would use a midwife to do that, because the hospitals and physicians will not do that unless the mother is about to die.

Otherwise it was illegal over there. So she asked the midwife to come over to where she was staying. He didn't know his wife did that. The midwife performed the abortion and left, and she bled to death or something.

The police wanted to know who committed the abortion, and then the café owner was interrogated. He said, "Well, all I know is she knows this woman and that woman," and so they found the lady and she went in jail.

One night when we were sitting there, I got up to get rid of my plate, and I left my purse there on the bench. So when I came back he told me, "You know, that ring around your finger, that's not real."

I said, "What do you mean?"

He said, "You're not married."

I said, "How do you know that?"

He said, "I went into your purse and looked at your identification card, and you're single."

I looked at him and said. "Really."

He shrugged and said, "Well, what can you do?"

I told him, "And don't you tell nobody, because I don't want nobody to know it. I can't handle all these guys around me, I have to tell them I'm married, or I knock them out."

Lud said to me, "I think I'm going to marry you." Bluntly like that.

He shocked me. I thought, "What does he want from me? I'm an old bag." I was five years older than him. Plus I worked my tutu off. I didn't see at that moment the future. I was thinking my whole life I had to work, work, work to survive. In my mind was surviving. So I didn't see any love or nothing. "What the hell am I going to do with that kid?" That's what I thought. I was used to all these older men. I thought I needed like a father type. Lud was not a father type. To me he was just a young kid, a boy, not a man. He was a nice person, but Lud was more like a brother to me. But I was surprised and flattered by that, and he was good looking. Most of the time most of them always marry the same people from Indonesia.

I was quiet and I looked at him, and I told him, "You're nuts. You're still green behind your ears." The Dutch expression is "green." I didn't want to hurt his feelings, because he seemed to be nice, so I said, "Well, I do have a boyfriend. He's at sea right now, but he's coming back."

CHAPTER THIRTY-FIVE

I'M NOT GOING TO GIVE UP ON YOU, THAT'S FOR SURE

I TOLD LUD WHAT MY FAMILY WAS LIKE, AND I SAID, "YOU DON'T want me. Look at the garbage I came from, I'm surrounded with," and all this heavy duty stuff. He just sat and listened.

I thought, "Why would he take me after all that I've been through?" You know what I mean? Nicolas wanted to live with me, but not marriage. Charles wanted to help me and did everything for me, but he never said, "Well, we're going to get married," either. But Lud didn't know what kind of load there was behind me, and I did not want to give that to him. Plus, I didn't want a dysfunctional family. I was not following my mother. I didn't want kids, period.

Lud told me, "You know what? If you need anything, I got money. Here's my wallet. Take whatever you want or need."

"Oh, no. That's not my custom," I said, "I'll ask you if I need something."

He said, "Oh, okay, fine."

Later Lud talked to his mom on the phone in Holland and told her about me. The leader of the Hawaiian band, his wife was living in the same town as Lud's mom, and the bandleader told his family that Lud had a relationship with a girl who worked at the same place they were, and he didn't think that she was a girl for him. Because meeting someone in a place like that, and to have a relationship like that was fine, but to marry, that was something else.

Lud had a friend in Amsterdam, Leo Rasso. When Lud had come from Indonesia to Holland, they found out he had tuberculosis, and they took him to a sanatorium with eight beds. Everything was open except the roof and right in the middle of pine trees. They put him there, and they put him flat on the bed, no medicine, nothing. Just strictly lying down for one year. Leo was there in the sanatorium also, so that's how Lud met him, and they became friends.

Leo was a Jewish boy, and talk about misery, that guy lost everything during the war. His mother was killed, his father was killed, his sister, and she was pregnant, all killed in a row by the Germans. He was not a healthy person, and he was in the hospital when the whole thing happened. He had curly hair, brown eyes, and a slender figure with real German Caucasian features, so they put him in girl's clothes, and they took him out as a girl, and nobody knew where he went. He went by his aunt, and she raised him.

When they got released from the sanatorium, Lud invited Leo over to the house, and he lived with his mom off and on. So after Lud told his mom about me, she sent Leo down to Antwerp to check up on Lud, what was going on. When I met Leo, I was scared, because he told me Lud's mother was not like me, and that's why he came over. He was sitting there with me one time, and I told him, "Well, I think when you hear about my family, you're not going to be that happy with me."

He said, "Yeah, I heard about it, but it has nothing to do with you."

So I said, "No, but I'm still her daughter," you know.

He said, "No, that is not what I see in you." So then we started talking about what happened to his family, and I hated what happened to him.

I was talking about angels, but I was Catholic, you know. I didn't know better. Leo told me, "I don't believe in God, I don't believe in angels, I don't believe in anything."

He became close friends with me. He went back and reported back to Lud's mom, but what he reported, I don't know. He never said anything bad from me, so far as I know.

Lud didn't tell me about his family at first, but when we were off for a couple of days, Lud told me, "I'm going to take you up to Amsterdam and meet my folks."

I said, "Well, I don't know. Do you think I should?"

He said, "Well, it's inevitable. Because I'm not going to give up on you, that's for sure."

That's what we did. Right after work, we hopped on the Amsterdam-Paris train. Lud said, "Don't worry about it. Even if they don't accept you, I accept you. It doesn't make any difference."

"Okay." And so I trusted him.

It was a long trip with a half-hour stop in the city of Breeda, on the border between Holland and Belgium to allow the border custom authorities and currency exchange agents to come aboard the train. Then the train went straight to the central train station in Amsterdam.

So we came there. His dad, John, was not home. He was a schoolteacher, out of state somewhere far away from home, reschooling all the people who came from Indonesia. So he came only once in the week home.

Lud's mother was real beautiful. He introduced me to her, and he told her, "Mom, I think this is the girl I'm going to marry." And his mom just stared at him.

Her name was Frieda. She was short and round, part Caucasian, part Asian features. She had been well-educated, but she didn't use it. She was just a home mom. She played quite well, and she was accompanied by Lud's dad on the violin. They played chamber music.

Lud's mom was like a little bird with the wings over him. Whatever came in the house was not good enough for Lud.

Lud's dad had an army cot, and Lud took it and spread it out in the living room. We slept there, we hugged, and we fell asleep, and when I woke up, his mom was sitting in front of us, just staring at us.

She called Lud aside and said, "Do you know what? This is not a girl for you."

Lud said, "Why not?"

"You can't afford her."

"What do you mean?"

She said, "The clothing, the underwear. She wears clothes from Fredrick's of Hollywood."

My shoes were high heels, with the little lace on top, and I was wearing black stockings with the lines in them.

Lud said, "I don't know."

His mom said, "You have to consider, this girl cannot cook for you."

He said, "Yeah, I thought about that."

She said, "You like Indonesian food."

Lud said, "I can learn to eat what she makes, and I can teach her something."

She said, "Oh, well, I don't think it's going to work out. But it is up to you."

CHAPTER THIRTY-SIX

WHERE'S YOUR HUSBAND?

LUD'S DAD, JOHN, HAD TRULY ASIAN FEATURES, DARK HAIR AND eyes. He was a very shy and timid person, but he was always very athletic and good at gymnastics.

In 1900, Lud's grandfather on his father's side, Johannes Buerman, who was Dutch, went out from Holland to Indonesia to work as a supervisor in charge of local military police. All the police he supervised were Indonesian. One of his officers married an Indonesian woman named Wagynam and the officer had two children with her and one on the way. What happened was, Johannes had an eye on Wagynam, but she was married to this officer. So Johannes sent the officer out on patrol and the officer "got killed." So Johannes then married Wagynam while she was pregnant with this third child.

Wagynam told stories, in her own language, which was the Indonesian language, about how she became a Christian. She was a regular Muslim. Johannes was a Christian, and he introduced his religion to her. But he left it like that. He never forced her, he never told her to go to church or anything.

She said she was sleeping one night, and she woke up and saw a vision of somebody very powerful standing in front of her surrounded by a lot of lights holding two books in his hands, one in the left hand, and one in the right. He was not saying anything. She said, "I remember seeing that one of the books had writing on it. The other one was blank."

She didn't know what it meant, and she woke up and told Johannes. Johannes said, "I think we should talk to one of the elders of the church, and maybe he can tell us what we missed."

According to Lud's grandma, this pastor told her, "Yeah, you're Muslim now, but you have come to this crossroads in your life. You must choose which way you want to go. You want to continue and follow your path, following the book with no writings on it, or you want to go where it's filled with good stuff?"

She said, "Yeah, I want to go where it's written."

"Well," he said, "that's the Christian faith, and you have to accept Christ Jesus as your Lord and Savior, and then after that we'll baptize you, and you'll be a Christian, and we'll give you a Christian name." So they christened her with the name "Elizabeth." So always after that time, her name was Elizabeth. She could not read. But she could hear, and she went to the Christian churches and they read the Bible to her.

When she gave birth to the officer's third child, even though it was not Johannes's son, he was given the name of "Buerman," and that was Lud's father, John.

Someone told Lud's dad that he had two brothers, but he never met them. He was raised as an only child. Johannes always showered him with rewards, and he was a lonesome introvert with no friends. They were living on the Island Sumba, which is a little island in the Archipelagos. He was always by himself, so Johannes gave him what he always wanted, a .22 caliber rifle.

After school he stayed out in the woods a long, long time and came home late at night sometimes with wild game he killed. He told stories about crawling in a small canoe, rowing down the rivers, and being surrounded by crocodiles. It didn't scare him or anything.

John was sent to Holland to a technical school called the Queen Wilhelmina. He was supposed to study there for four years and finish school for his degree in Electrical Engineering. He did it in two years flat with honors.

Lud's grandfather on his mother's side, Emmett, was also Dutch. Emmett went to Indonesia at a young age. He was working for a company, making maps for Indonesia, and he had this Indonesian woman named Tjo cleaning his clothes and shining his boots and cooking for him. After the third child with her, Emmett married her. That's where Lud's mom, Frieda, came from. Frieda was the youngest of two boys and three girls, and I think she lost her mom, Tjo, when she was thirteen years old.

Lud's dad never told me how he and Frieda met, but I believe that Johannes and Emmett got together and they said, "Hey, maybe your daughter and my son should get to know each other." In those days, you had to marry a girl of your standards. As a man, you got to be able to show what you're worth, academically, or professionally, or moneywise. So John was good academically, and he was still young so he couldn't say, "Well, I'm rolling in the bucks." But he had a future; that is why he was allowed to meet with Frieda.

They married in 1933. They lived in Indonesia, had five children, and two died.

Lud was born in 1934, and he had a sister who was a year younger than him named Evadne. They were very close to one another, because he had no siblings other than her for awhile. So growing up they did a lot of things together. She was still living with her mom and dad when I met them. She took more after

Lud's dad; a very quiet, shy person. Evadne was very religious. She worked most of the time as a clerk in an office, and when she was off she was either in church or in her room.

Lud's younger sister Daisy came another three or four years after Lud and Evadne. She was not like Evadne at all. She liked to go to parties, she liked to dance, she liked to sing, she got a good voice. At the time I first met the family, Daisy was sixteen years old and she was having a relationship with a man who was twenty-seven, I think. That relationship was really, really trouble as far as Lud's parents were concerned. She had dropped out of school, and she was no longer living at the house, but the parents of this man took her in.

Lud's mom and dad were Dutch citizens, and he was working for the Dutch government for the electric company on high tension wires in a colony in the Indonesian Archipelago. He put up the cables and the posts in the ground, and he did that for a long time. When the war broke out, he enlisted in the Royal Dutch Indonesian Army, and he was stationed in Ground Anti-Aircraft Division.

I remember him telling me that in 1941 when the Japanese flew in, and the Dutch went to their cannons, they found out it was sabotage. They couldn't aim, they couldn't do nothing. So his commanding officer told him, "Just throw your weapons away and surrender."

At the time Lud was only seven years old, Evadne was five, and Daisy, three. They lived not too far away from the airport. What happened was, they knew the Japanese were invading Indonesia, so they were expecting something was going to happen. All of a sudden they heard planes flying over, and Lud looked out. The Japanese had these Zeros, fast planes, and the Dutch air force had those clunky double-deckers with the Tommy guns trying to shoot. They didn't have a chance. You could see that. The Japanese were playing around them, you know, and finally they sent every one of the Dutch planes down to the ground. After that the bombs came. They dropped bombs on the airfield so no one could take off. And the following day, sure enough, there were trucks coming in with all these Japs, and they stopped and they got out of the trucks, and they came into the house. The officer asked Lud's mom, he said, "Where's your husband?"

Frieda said, "My husband is not here."

And he said, "Where is he?"

She said, "Well, I don't know,"

He said, "Do you have any weapons?"

His mom said, "No." And he had his soldiers search the house, under the mattress; they found nothing. So they went back outside, but they didn't move. The trucks stayed there. So two hours, three hours went by, and they came back and went through their kitchen. They took eggs, green onions, rice, they put it in pots and pans, they grabbed it, went back to their trucks, and then they continued.

They didn't know what happened to Lud's dad. They heard that the Japanese were going to have a troop transport of POWs through the street where he lived, and they were warned not to go out there and watch it and observe it, because these Japanese don't like that. So Lud's mom got herself a parasol and stood on the side of the road while these trucks were going by with all of these POWs in the back, and there came these Japanese soldiers walking in the street. One of the soldiers, a small one, spotted Lud's mom under the umbrella. He was yelling at her in Japanese, "Get off the street!" and gave her a big whack. She was stunned and fell on her butt, you know, and Lud saw that. As a child he felt like jumping on the guy and choking him to death. But what can you do? They told them not to watch, but Lud's mom did it in hope to find out if John was alive. Was he one of them on the big transport? She didn't see him in the trucks full of soldiers, with all the faces going by.

Lud's mom took the kids and moved in with her father, Emmett, and they tried to survive that way, and for three and a half years they didn't know if they still had a dad. Was he a prisoner of war in Indonesia, Asia, Japan? They had hope. They hoped and prayed that he was still alive.

CHAPTER THIRTY-SEVEN

I'M NOT GOING BACK TO INDONESIA

IN INDONESIA LIFE WAS DIFFERENT, BECAUSE EVERYTHING WAS occupied by the Japanese, and controlled by the Japanese, and regulated by the Japanese. They had the police headquarters across the street, and when the Japs came in, all the policemen were still there, and they were still functioning as a police force, but under Japanese rules.

The Japanese just treated the Indonesians like natives, laborers, and people who were selling stuff. They were tolerant of them, they accepted them the way their lifestyles were, and they gave them their space, whatever they needed. It was the Dutch people the Japanese were after, because the Dutch were allies of the United States. They were not hostile toward Lud's family, because they blended there with the Indonesians. But the average Indonesians walked around there in slippers or bare feet, and as Lud was Dutch descent, they were always taught to have shoes on. So the Japanese could pick the Dutch out. Sometimes they asked questions, and they had to carry an ID and show them they were Dutch that lived there for a long time.

Lud's family didn't know anything. They couldn't have a radio. It was against the law. They couldn't even get bicycle tires. The only thing they could get were the "dead" inner tubes. There was no air in them, it was just this ring of solid rubber, and you put it around the wheel of your bicycle.

Lud's mother worked in the kitchen, she cared for her father, for her kids. Before the war, she had a cook, she had a cleaning lady, she had a yard lady. She was rich there. Then the servants had to leave them. They would be killed otherwise.

At that time, Lud was eight or nine years old, and he did part-time jobs to get money to buy food, loading and unloading trucks with cowhides, putting them in a warehouse. Lud was only average size, but they didn't care. They needed labor. He got forty cents for each cow hide, but he wanted to make more money so he carried two at a time, sometimes three, and he hurt himself and got a hernia. But he never told anyone at that age, because he knew that they would keep him from going out and making money.

All the schools closed, except the Japanese schools. But then you had to learn the Japanese language. The first thing they did was they had the kids stand in line, and then they said the pledge of allegiance, they faced the sun east, and they bowed three times. After that they went to class, and they had to say the Japanese alphabet. Lud had to learn to write this. If he wanted to spell his name, he could not spell it in Japanese; he had to make all kinds of symbols, and to them that sounded like "Buerman." Buerman was maybe a little house with some lines and a roof and so on. Lud got sick of this, so he said, "Okay, forget it. I'm not going to learn this language."

So Lud's mom managed to get him into a Catholic school, because every government benefit school shut down. But he was not long in the Catholic school because after maybe a year, they wanted you to become Catholic. Lud's family was Protestant, and he didn't like that, so he said, "Forget it." But after the occupation that's all you could get.

Lud and his sisters were introduced to Sunday school while Indonesia was still in the Japanese occupation. They had private Sunday schools, and since that time Lud's sister Evadne never missed church.

When the Japs surrendered, Lud's mother contacted the Red Cross to find out if John Buerman was alive, if they knew where he was. It took about a month, and she got a letter back from the Red Cross: "Yes, we found him. He is in Manila with the relief." The Americans took him to the Philippines to feed him, to bring him up. He was going to be transported back to Indonesia to Balikpapan in the Island Borneo, and if she liked they could arrange for her and the kids to be in Borneo to meet with him.

The day of the Japanese attack, Lud's dad was captured and taken away to a prison camp in Hakodate, Japan for three and a half years.

In the camp, the Japanese were looking for all kinds of metal, copper, gold. If you had gold teeth, they'd probably pull them out, and if you were wearing a wedding ring they'd take it off your finger. Lud's dad told Lud, "That was a symbol of marriage to your mother, so I swallowed it. I thought the next day I could probably fish it back out again and they would forget about the whole thing by then." And sure enough he fished it out and put it back on his finger.

The Japanese had a lot of Dutch and Americans also as prisoners who were sick. And when you're sick, your rations are cut in less than half. Lud's dad was a good blacksmith, and the Japanese needed big hooks for the trains. So Lud's dad volunteered and said, "I can make it if you have the equipment to heat the iron. Give me an anvil and a hammer and I will make the hooks for you." He did it out of nothing, and they were so surprised that they gave him recognition in the Japanese force. For what he did, he got the best food, and extra food whatever he could eat, and he shared it with the people who were sick and needed that.

The Americans came into Japan, and Lud's dad told stories about being surrounded by barbed wire. They heard a rumble, and these American big tanks were approaching the camp. The tanks rolled right over the gates, and just kept going. He said, "I could not describe the sight, the excitement of seeing the Americans." He said when they came out of the tanks, they were young, big guys, and they gave them food.

After the war, the British marched into Indonesia and some other soldiers from other countries. There were soldiers from India, and Mongolians, I don't know where they came from, but they stayed just until the Dutch government could get back on its feet, then they moved out and everything fell back into the Dutch rules, you know.

In the city where Lud lived there was no damage to buildings or anything. Everything just ran its course. Transportation was the same, hospitals were still operating, everything opened up again; private schools, Catholic schools, the Christian schools, the high schools, and everything started running again.

Indonesia was one of the Dutch colonies for 350 years before the Japanese moved in. So there was all this friction between the Indonesian people and the Dutch government. But then when the Japanese came and took over, the Indonesians thought, "This is an ally for us to get our freedom."

Five years after Japan surrendered they had a round-table conference, of all the nations, I think, and the United States told the Dutch people, "Get out of there and give the Indonesians their freedom." So in 1950 Indonesia obtained their independence. All the people who were under the Indonesians could either become Indonesian citizens or leave the country. In order to become Indonesian citizens there's a lot of questions you ask yourself. You say, "Well, what's this nation going to do? Is it going to survive? Is it going to become a third world country or what?" Lud's dad thought, "Well, if they knew we were somehow descended from the Dutch or connected with the Dutch, then they would treat us as outcasts and second-class citizens."

Lud was then fifteen. Lud's family were always Dutch citizens, so his dad said, "You know what? I have a half-year paid vacation coming, so we're going to spend our vacation in Holland." But once they were there in Holland he told the government, "I'm not going back to Indonesia unless I become an Indonesian citizen." He said, "We're not going to take a chance and we're going to remain in Holland." He was not anticipating trouble, because he studied in Holland himself. He never told them that it was an issue with their skin color.

Holland at that time was being swamped by all the Dutch descended coming in, so Holland became overcrowded. The housing was bad; you had to stay on a waiting list for two or three years to get something. At that time, New Guinea was split up. One side belonged to Australia, and one side belonged to the Netherlands, and Lud's family was thinking of going over there and starting anew, you know. But it never happened.

Lud finished his school in Holland. There were a lot of problems about them being in Holland, because when you say you're Dutch, they expected you to have blue eyes and blonde hair, and at least white skin. And he don't have that. He couldn't change the color of his eyes, couldn't make them blue, couldn't make his hair blond. There were lots of fights. They told him to go back where he came from, "You're taking our jobs away." He was called a "Chinaman," a "Peanut man," and you name it.

His sisters never talked about being harassed because of their color. Just the boys for some reason. But Lud hated Holland, and that's why he left.

CHAPTER THIRTY-EIGHT

HE DON'T WANT YOU

AFTER THAT FIRST MEETING WITH LUD'S FAMILY, WE WENT back to Antwerp. The only time we saw each other was at work, because I delivered telegrams during the day. Lud slept for a couple hours, and then rehearsed with the band for the next night.

After about two weeks, Lud said, "Get your papers ready, because I'm going to marry you, and you're going to be living with me here in Holland. Not Belgium."

We lost our jobs, because there was no secret no more. We came in together, and it was noticed by the boss. Marcus said, "What's going on here?"

Lud said, "Don't worry. I know we can't stay here. We're going to get married."

One night when I came in, one of the girls said, "Rach, Nicolas was here from the ship." Nicolas came in during the day when I was not there, but somebody told him I worked there.

I thought, "Oh shoot."

"He went to your apartment and he didn't find you," she said. The apartment was empty; I was not there, so he started looking. The ship foreman whose daughters I worked with delivering telegrams told Nicolas, "Oh, she's working at the Oberbayhren."

I told Lud right away, "Listen, Nicolas might come in, and then I have to leave, because otherwise there's going to be a big battle here." And then he did come in.

I was working, Lud was playing, and then Nicolas asked me, "Where the hell did you go? The bird died. What happened? Did you go to Ghent?"

I forgot all about the bird, because I was not used to the bird.

I said, "No, I didn't. I met somebody, and I stayed with him." I didn't say nothing about who the guy was, because Lud was on a special work permit, and certainly he was dark, so there was a second problem there.

Then Nicolas said, "No way."

I said, "Yeah."

He said, "You don't going to do that to me."

I said, "You did it to me, and you lied to me."

He said, "Well, you better come over and get your things, because I'm leaving the apartment."

I said, "Okay."

So the next day I went to the apartment, and then Nicolas had a fight with me, because he found out who I was engaged to. He said, "You're not going to marry that guy. He's a kid. Are you nuts or something? He don't want you. He lives in Holland, and knowing you, you're not going to be happy there." So he said to me, "You better think it over."

Then he grabbed me, and I thought, "Uh oh, he's going to rape me or something."

"Don't touch me," I told him, "Because I'm pregnant."

I could see it scared him. He was in shock. He thought, "What the hell?" He said, "How can you get pregnant? You can't!" and a whole bunch of things. Then he took me on the bed, made some hickies on my neck, took my clothes away, and he said, "Here! Go to him now and see what he says."

Nicolas thought that because Lud was from Holland, and because he was from Indonesia, he would see me like that and throw me out.

So I put on my coat and took the streetcar, and I went back to Lud at the hotel. I opened my coat and said, "Here I am."

Lud said, "What happened?"

I said, "He took my clothes."

Lud held me tight, hugged me and kissed me and said, "Let's go buy you some clothes."

That night, Nicolas brought back my clothes, and then he asked to dance with me. I said, "For what? I don't want to dance."

"Yeah," he said, "I want to have the last dance."

"Okay. But you ask Lud. I'm not going to dance with you if he don't like it."

Nicolas asked Lud, "Can I have a last dance with her?"

Lud said, "Sure."

"Can you play the song, 'Because of You'?"

"Sure."

After the dance, Nicolas reached out and grabbed Lud's hand. "Listen," he said. "Promise me one thing. If you ever get tired of her, even if she has a baby, send her back to me."

"Yeah," Lud said.

In Nicolas's mind he still thought Lud was going to dump me. Because he knew my past, and he hated my stepfather and my mother. And he turned ugly. But then he didn't have what he wanted. That is where you learn about the guy. And he wasn't the nice guy I took him for.

I was older then. But wherever I worked, I always met with Inspector Beck, we saw each other for a cup of coffee or some-thing. I was in an apartment when he came for the last time, and he told me, "Now I'm going to say goodbye, because you are no longer that age and I trust you. I hear that you are going to go away."

I said, "Yes, but don't tell nobody because I'm making my papers ready. I am going to go to Holland and get married."

He said, "You did a good job. I'm proud of you. You can stand on your own legs."

After that Lud and I packed our clothes and we left for Amsterdam real quick, because Lud didn't want to meet up with Nicolas again.

CHAPTER THIRTY-NINE

I LOST EVERYTHING

I WANTED TO SHOW LUD MY FOLKS BEFORE I LEFT FOR HOLLAND, because it was on my mind that once I left Belgium, I was never going back. I said, "I want you to see my parents. I wouldn't be surprised if you dumped me after that."

Lud said, "You can take me anywhere you want. I don't care if they walk upside down and have eyeballs growing out of the middle of their foreheads. I'm going to marry you," he said.

So he met them. Then he found out my mother played cards all day. The apartment was a mess, was filthy, was dirty. Geoff was in and out, fooling around with my sister. Lud couldn't carry on a conversation with my mother or Geoff. But it didn't bother Lud. He told me his first impression was that my mother was like a plant. You look at her, she exists, and that is it. He told me the one thing that he noticed first was that she had a lot of warts on her face, and he thought to himself, "If you just removed those warts, you'd be a better looking woman."

Before we got married, we had to go to Belgium to city hall and ask for my papers. Then in Belgium you had to be twenty-five to get married without parental consent, and I was only twenty-three. We wrote, and my mother didn't sign the papers, so then we wrote my uncle Michiel. Michiel went to my mother, and there was a whole bedonia there. He told her, "You better help your daughter and get the damn thing done," so my mother finally did. Then she couldn't find Caluwaerts, the guy that gave me the stupid name, so it was dragging out like crazy. I sold my jewelry, and with the money I got a lawyer, and he found Caluwaerts. So six months it took us waiting to get married.

In the meantime, I lived with Lud's mom and dad there in Holland in their little two-bedroom apartment, and Lud started looking for jobs; two weeks here, two weeks there. He finally settled into repairing office machines. While all this was going on, I could not stay in Holland longer than three months. Holland was a foreign country as far as Belgium was concerned. So I had to go back to Belgium, re-register, and then go another three months.

I never saw the Bible until I met Lud's dad. I was a Catholic. In my time, the Catholics was on the top. You couldn't say nothing against them, so I kept my mouth long shut. I didn't talk too much about churches, because sometimes people had a different idea, so I don't want it to be a hang-up to our friendship. John, he was a sweetheart. He brought me a beautiful little Dutch Bible from Holland. I still have it. It was my first Bible. I was looking in that Bible, and I thought, "Wow, what happened?" I thought, "I'm never going to come out of it." Now I'm okay, but then in the beginning, I had a feeling evil was constantly around me.

Lud's mom and dad had Bible school in the house every Wednesday. A few people from the church, they came over, the minister came, his daughters, they all sat around the table. I sat in sometimes and I followed it, and that's where I started learning the Bible. My father-in-law said, "Start in the New Testament when Jesus died, don't start with the Old."

I thought, "Why only half of the book?"

Lud saw it different. He said, "No, you have to have the whole thing."

So we went over it, me and him. Lud knew, and he explained it real good to me so I understood it.

My mother-in-law was not an angel, I tell you that. So long as I was not married, I could not go out and work. So Lud's mom said, "When you're here, you can do the cleaning."

In Indonesia before the war, she didn't have to do nothing. She couldn't clean, she was used to maids and cooks. Cooking she learned from her maid in Indonesia. I did the beds; I was used to that. But then she said, "No, we don't make up the beds like this."

Well, I learned to make beds for a long time. I said, "How do you want it?"

"I want my linen folded this way and this way. You have the right side so far off the ground, and the left side that way." Then when I got that done, and I did Evadne's room, she said, "Well, this and this and this and this."

I said, "Okay," so I did what she said.

She wouldn't talk to you if you didn't do it right. In other words, if she couldn't get her way the normal way by asking, she played dirty. She said to Lud, "Look at that, your wife don't wash her clothes. She lets it stack up for a whole week."

Lud said, "Well, so what?"

She said, "It's better if she washes it every day just a little bit."

Then Lud came to me, "Mama said it's better to wash it every day just a little bit."

Then she told Lud, "Your wife is using too much hot water and soap."

Lud said, "You said you want her to wash it every day."

"Yeah, but this and that." She watched me every second, and it drove me up the wall. Every time, "This is too much, this is too short, this is too long."

Then she wouldn't cook for me. She said, "Well, you don't eat Asian food. Tell Lud to buy you bread." So Lud bought me French bread, and that's what I lived on.

When I was alone, and she went shopping or something, I sat down and prayed. Then I thought to myself, "It's stupid that I'm sitting here waiting to get married to him. Why is it that I let everything go?" When I was in Belgium I got jobs, I got everything I wanted. What the hell happened to me? I lost everything.

Lud's sisters worked at the bank, so I didn't see them that often, but sometimes on the weekends they came over. They were first a little bit distant. They always thought people didn't like them because they were oriental. That's bull. I never had that attitude to nobody.

The oldest one, Evadne, she was nice to me, but when the mother said something, she would change the attitude. Evadne was always mommy's girl; "Whatever Mommy says, Mommy's right." Some girls hang more on their mother than is supposed to be, you know. Sometimes it is not good to do that, and I was the "bad" girl.

My mother-in-law told me, "Well, you should be a virgin when you're married."

Well, I was not a virgin. "I'm sorry," I told her, "not everybody can be perfect." That's what I told her.

Daisy, the younger one, she was always more open to me. She called me in, and she told me stories. She said, "Don't be afraid from Mom. She's telling you that story from virgin, but she was not a virgin when she married, either."

I was miserable. I cried a river many, many times. I said to Lud, "I've had it. I'm going back to Belgium."

Lud said, "How are we going back to Belgium? We've got no money. We've got nothing."

While Lud was working, I thought I'd go to the station and see if I could get somebody that would pay my way back to Belgium, and there I could work again. Lud came home and couldn't find me, so he got his bicycle and rode around, and there I was walking. He said, "What do you think you're doing?"

"I'm going back to Belgium."

"Walking?"

"Yeah."

"Come on. Without a suitcase? Without nothing?"

I said, "I don't give a shit."

CHAPTER FORTY

FOUR MIRACLES

O<small>NCE</small> I <small>GOT MY PAPERS</small>, I <small>WAS RELEASED FROM</small> B<small>ELGIUM</small>. T<small>HE</small> wedding announcement had to be posted in public outside on the City Hall bulletin board for six weeks. You could be married before, or you could be a criminal, and everybody can see who's married, who's not.

We didn't know what we were getting into. Was it a good thing, was it a bad thing, should we do it or not? Lud told his mom, "Look, if I don't get your blessing and you don't consent to the fact that I'm marrying this girl, I will return to Belgium with her and marry her there. It's okay with me."

"Oh no," she said. "I want you to marry here, and I'll make her wedding dress." And you know it came out quite nice. It was simple, a long skirt, a nice blouse over, and then she made a little hat with a veil over it. She made it right to my size, you know. Simple and cheap.

The ceremony was in the city hall in Amsterdam. I didn't have my family. A city official came, and he looked and looked, and he asked me, "Do you have anyone to give the bride away?"

I said, "No, nobody's here."

So he hugged me and he said, "Well, I will." And he did.

Lud rented a tuxedo with a top hat. He was nervous about the whole thing. Neither of us had ever been married before. I remember he kept looking at me. I was so scared. I had a bouquet in my left hand, I think, and I put my arm around his, and he almost dragged me in.

After the wedding I was still scared. I thought, "I'm going to not make it, I'm going to not make it." Because I was not used to marriage. Well, my uncles were all married and were happy, but I thought, "I don't see a happy marriage from my mother, so maybe I'm going to go through the same thing." But then Lud took me through it. It was not like we had roses right away. We didn't have fights, but we talked about things, and I had to learn a lot from the Indonesian side.

There was no houses, because of the influx of the Asians immigrating or going back to Holland, so we lived with Lud's parents. But it wasn't as bad as before, because I could finally go back to work. I worked first in a factory where they made cookies. There I got some problems, because Lud was Indonesian, and they didn't like that I was married with him. I said, "I'm coming here for a job, and I'm not going to talk about my marriage. It is not your business." So I quit. I said, "Hey, I don't go here to be offended."

Then I did my own business. I thought, "Well, that's better." I started with another girl sewing lamp shades. Then we began cleaning apartments, and when that took off we hired other people. We worked for companies in Amsterdam, cleaning the offices in the evening, and I made good money. I made more than Lud, because in Holland you are paid for your age, and he was younger.

I can tell you hundreds of miracles in my life. Lud's mother wanted a baby. So I checked it out, that I was okay, because I knew I was not normal with my menstruation. Well, I got that problem from the camp, I think. Lud's cousin, Hans, was a professor in Holland. He talked to me after the wedding, and he helped me with the pictures. The family was fantastic to me, and they all were beautiful people. He told me, "I'm going to send you to a specialist that I know, and he can find out." So I went to the specialist in Holland, and he said, "The womb is closed and you can't have kids."

I said, "Oh, thank you, Lord. I don't want to have kids." I didn't plan on it, and I told Lud that. I was scared. I raised my brother and my sister and I thought, "I don't think I'm a good mother." I don't think I was ready. But the doctor told me he could perform an operation that would fix the problem.

It was stupid, but my mother-in-law was really upset because Lud was the only boy in the family to carry on the name. My two sisters-in-law they don't count because they don't have the name. So my mother-in-law was telling me, "Oh, and I need that, and I need more grandkids, and I need this and that," and she was hanging on like crazy, you know.

Well, Lud left it up to me. Lud didn't care. He said, "Whatever you want. It's not up to my mother."

But then I felt so sad, and so I said, "Okay." She wanted only one. But I didn't know if I was going to have a boy or a girl.

I saw the doctor and he said he would make me ready for the operation. I came back to his clinic there in Amsterdam, and my mother-in-law was with me. Then the doctor went to work on it. I don't know what the heck he did, but it was painful that was for sure. Then I got shots again. About six months later I started slowly bleeding, and then I didn't stop bleeding. So the doctor said, "Uh oh. We have to check it again." So we checked it again, and then he gave me some shots again, and I was bleeding again. It came and it went.

Lud's mom was raised Protestant, and we went by the Pentecostal church in Holland, where they are speaking in tongues, you know. Oh my goodness, what a difference that was from the Catholics. The pastor was from Indonesia, too. Pastor Diese was his name. So when we went they asked, "Who wants to be baptized?"

Lud's parents told me if I wanted to make it in life, I had to be baptized. And I thought, "Baptized? I am baptized." But something came over me and I thought, "Maybe you should get baptism." So I told Lud maybe we should go.

So I went to the baptism. Pastor Diese made us ready, me and Lud together. I went in that pool, and I thought, "Oh my God, they're going to see I'm bleeding." But they didn't, and I was baptized. Then the bleeding stopped instantly, and it never came back. Isn't that funny? A lot of people thought I'm stupid or sick or that was not true, but it happened to me, and I never got problems again. I thought, "That's it. That's a sign." That was the first miracle to me that I understood.

Well, I went home, and the doctor fixed me up with some shots in the morning, and then later he came back and checked it out. Then I have to go back to the other doctor and he checked it out, and it looked fine to him. So he said, "I bet everything is perfect. It is clean, and it is open, so you should be ready to have a baby." And I was and I did.

I was scared there, too, because I thought, "Oh my God, I'm going to have it," you know. So I thought, "I hope the baby is okay," in my mind. I said to the Lord, "Please let it be healthy." I was really not ready for a baby at all, because I was scared.

So finally around four months the doctor told me not to work no more, because he was scared I would lose the baby. I was real weak, and I couldn't lift no more. Lud was working then already for an Italian typewriter company in Amsterdam.

Well, they checked me out. We didn't have all the luxury that we have now that you can see on the machine. They had to do that testing feeling with the hands, and it hurts. The doctor told me everything looked beautiful, the baby looked okay, they said. Except maybe I was too small to deliver the baby.

When I was young, I was really small and tiny. It wasn't a big baby, was seven pounds, but I was real small. They thought I was so heavy that the baby couldn't pass through my bones, they had to open me, and all this. When the doctor told me that, right away I went back to my Father. And I was praying like hell by myself. I just talked to Jesus like I'm talking to you, and I said, "You want me to have the baby?" If not I wouldn't have the baby.

Then the next miracle happened. When it came time to deliver the baby, I went to the hospital in Amsterdam, Holland. It was a special building connected to the hospital where the births are. I had to be in there for eight days, because they were scared from the bleeding. The doctor said, "Well, you are ready. I'm going to get a cup of coffee, and then I'll be back and perform the operation." So he went out the door, and so soon he went out the door, I felt this pain in my back, and I was all alone.

You are in this big ward, and they put more people there. There was like a blanket partition that you can't see them, but you can hear them. I don't think it is like that no more, but I am talking about 1955. You had to be real quiet and not wake people up. And that is not easy when you deliver a baby, I tell you. So I said, "Sister!" to a nun. "Sister, I think something is wrong with me!" I never had a baby before, so I don't know what happened.

She said, "Shh," and she looked and she saw, and there came the baby.

And I told the nurse, "What you want me to do?"

She said, "Well, do it quietly." She got me something in my mouth that I can bite on so I don't scream, and I just kept it in. The doctor came right back, and he delivered my son. I was supposed to be operated on at two o'clock at night, and guess what? The baby came at 12 o'clock. So that was another miracle to me.

Then I started bleeding like hell, and the boy turned yellow, so they had to take him away and give him a blood transfusion. Then they took me out, and they gave me some shots. I was an RH factor patient. I had some sort of chemical in my blood that rejected my child.

I was scared, so I started praying again. "Lord, help us here." Because I was alone. Lud couldn't come by me there. At that time in Holland they don't allow it.

So later, after the crisis was over, the doctor said to me, "You are so blessed." He said, "Most of the time your case are miscarriages." So that why I knew the Lord was on my side.

The nurse said, "You got to watch your child. He's going to turn yellow. If it doesn't go away in twenty-four hours, call me, we have to rush him to the hospital."

I didn't tell nobody, but I said, "Lord, it is your baby. I give him back to you. You bless him." I don't have no idea what it was, but he came out of it, and everything just went perfect. The doctors checked him out, and he was a beautiful guy. He had no problem whatsoever.

It was funny. Charles told me I would never be able to have children. I told you, I believe in miracles. I was blessed, believe me, and after that I got pregnant again. I didn't predict that, because I wanted only one, but I told the Lord, "You want me to have it, and then I have it." And I did. My second son was born in May 1958 in Amsterdam.

My sister-in-law Evadne always had her babies home and she told me to stay home and have a natural birth there in the house with a midwife. She said, "Then Lud can stay with you."

So I told Lud, "I'm so scared because the doctor told me, 'Don't stay home, don't stay home, because your body is not good.'"

Lud said, "Well, everything goes perfect with the first one."

So I said, "Okay, I'll try to stay home."

Well, that was the wrong decision. I should've taken my own intuition.

The midwife came. She was really young, and the nurse was late when I went into labor. In the meantime, Lud's parents had a Bible class going on in the other room. My mother-in-law locked the outer door, but I could hear them, you know. Well, that was just the beginning. That kid was stuck. I was so weak I couldn't get him out, and the dumb midwife fainted. And guess what happened? Lud and my father-in-law, they had to help me to get the baby out. I was so scared and screaming, I was in horrible pain. My father-in-law was in shock, but he helped me real good, and Lud was there, but at that moment when everything went fiasco, there came the nurse in and she helped me with Lud and my father-in-law and delivered my boy. I was scared that he would die. But he came out normal and beautiful and everything. I never did that again. I said, "No more." Next time, I go to the hospital, and I listen to the doctors, not the stupid sister-in-law. That was a miracle, too, my God. You don't believe me, but I'm a miracle woman.

Then I didn't want kids no more. But I had another miracle ten years later in 1966. I'm happy that I did have them. The Lord blessed me with three beautiful boys.

My life was like a blessing. It was the best thing that ever happened, because whatever I did afterwards, I married Lud, I got the baby, and it was like heaven opened for me.

CHAPTER FORTY-ONE

I CAN'T SPEAK ENGLISH, BUT I'M GOING TO AMERICA

Holland was already overcrowded. There were no houses. You had to be on a waiting list, and all kinds of stuff. We finally got a three-bedroom apartment to live in. At that time in Holland, the gas and the electric were supplied by coin-operated meters. So for our gas and our lights we bought special pennies and then we dropped them into the machine that sat back by the water tank. There was no backyard, because we were on the third floor, and every time the kids wanted to play they had to go out on the sidewalk. Lud was hanging out the window watching our two poor boys playing on the sidewalk, dodging people walking back and forth, and he said, "This is no future for them. I've got to do something."

During the 1950s, leaflets were dropped around Amsterdam about emigration. Lud first started looking into Australia, because he always felt he'd like to contribute something he knew and something he could do to a new development. The letter came back saying that, based on their evaluation of Lud's grand-parents and mother and father, he didn't have enough Caucasian ancestors, and under the "White Australia" policy there was no quota for his skin color. Lud got so mad that he threw every-thing in the trash can and never talked about it again. Then Lud thought, "Maybe I should go to Brazil." They told him Brazil was very poor, and unless you are physically strong to work on farms, you don't have a chance there. He said, "Well, forget that. Let's go try for the Unites States." He thought back then the United States was only around 160 years old, "This is a new country. Maybe I can contribute and do something."

Because Holland was overcrowded, the Immigration and Nationality Act of 1952 was amended in 1958 with a special pro-vision for Dutch refugees, and they opened up a quota, so that people could come into the United States under the Pastor-Wal-ter Act and the Church World Service organization. Pastor and Walter were United States senators that had just passed the act in 1956 to allow for 3,000 families outside the regular quotas to come to the United States.

Lud filled out applications at the emigration office to see if he qualified, if they would accept him as a refugee, because he was considered a refugee coming from Indonesia. We sent the papers in, and they responded to the letter. I was a different quota, because I was from Belgium. I could come in as a regular immigrant. We were married, so we had a little problem there. But that was okay. It all got worked out, and in the end it don't make any difference.

We went twice to the American Consulate in Rotterdam. They checked out our records, and all the papers were clean. In those times you could not come over if you weren't, and if you did come over you could not hang on the government. We had to stand on our own feet, and we agreed with that. You know, we both knew how to work.

In the evenings, the American Consul presented classes in Amsterdam, and they told us what to do and what not to do in America. The guy could speak both languages. They let us see how America lives, and what they do, what food they had. So they showed us a movie and we saw the big stores and everything. We were hungry in Holland. So I said to Lud, "I don't give a shit what happens. I can't speak English, but I'm going to America with all that food." I said, "Hey, I'll do anything."

They told us, "One thing, if you do go, bring your tools with you."

Lud said, "Well, what tools are you talking about?"

"The tools you need. The backbone, and the language, and your hands."

The only thing I had problems with is I couldn't speak the language. Lud picked it up fast, but not me. I didn't like too much English. I liked the German and French better, and Lud said, "You better get serious, because you need that."

So I said, "Okay, I'll learn it." And I did. But not that good as he did. I still don't speak it right like you, believe me. But people understand me. I get away with it, I guess.

Meanwhile, they found sponsors for us, Jeanne Lee and Dr. Lydia Emery, and we were already writing letters to them. We were sponsored by the Oregon Methodist church. The Methodist church sponsored immigrants and refugees in California and the west coast through the Church World Service. Wherever a Methodist church was, people would be sponsored, you know.

A lot of people took the boat. Lud said, "No, that will take forever; I don't want to do that to the kids," so we took the plane all the way to New York. Well, the first time I saw New York I was in shock. It was so big, and the restaurants were so big, and we had a special pin on that said we were refugees. We had to stop over in New York, and from there we went to Chicago, from

Chicago we drove all the way to Vancouver, and from there we took a little train to Portland, Oregon. My sponsor Jeanne and Dr. Emery was there to pick us up with the car.

We arrived in Yoncalla, Oregon, between Eugene and Roseburg, in October 1961. I think at that time Yoncalla only had a population of 217, something like that.

I have a picture of Dr. Emery in uniform. She was a doctor in the navy during WWII, stationed in the Pacific, I think. I remember reading an article in an old Readers Digest about Dr. Emery. All the way up until she retired, she only charged $1.00 for patient visits. Dr. Emery herself was Methodist, and she was in the choir. She was a doctor for kids, so she helped my kids, got them shots, everything that they needed.

Jeanne was married to the Yoncalla Postmaster, Eldon Lee. Jeanne had just built a new house, so we moved into Jeanne's old house next door. The house was fantastic to me after that tiny apartment in Holland. It had a big, huge living room, a dining room, a big kitchen, and two bedrooms. We had a pot stove in the dining room, and in the back was a washer and dryer.

At church they gave us a great big Thanksgiving dinner. Dr. Emery was with me, and in the middle of the table was a big, huge turkey. I didn't know what a turkey looked like, so I told Dr. Emery, "I never saw a chicken that big!"

She said to me, "It's not a chicken. It's a turkey."

Jeanne said, "Gobble, gobble," to me. "Gobble, gobble." I don't care what she said; I never saw a turkey before.

So finally the day after she took me to some farm and she showed me what a turkey looked like. I felt so stupid, you know.

People came over to the house and helped me out. In America they had a washer and dryer. I was in shock because I did my wash all my life with just my hands. So they helped me with the wash, and cooking and baking American style. Dr. Emery came in the house, and then she explained how to put the stove on, high or low, the water, hot and cold.

We did a home study for English. What surprised me was, when the kids landed over here, they never thought of English. They learned it so fast, and they communicated with other kids. It's like they had been here all their life.

A week or two after we arrived there, they had a meeting, and all the members were sitting there and they had the blackboard there, and Lud had to get up and tell people why he emigrated to the United States. I remember one guy asked him, "So you are actually from Indonesia originally?"

"Yes."

"Why do they have this brown skin color?"

Well, Lud couldn't answer him. So he said, "Well, because the sun shines more than it does here in your place. We develop something in our skin to prevent it from burning up." And everybody just laughed. He didn't know what else to tell them.

I really was treated so good. People brought food every day. I was shocked about that, because the people would knock on the door, and it was all open all the time, and they came in and called my name, "Rachel!" and they always had something for me. The sheriff, Melvin, he was really nice. He was an Indian, big huge tall guy. He had a ranch with beautiful horses, and he would come in and take the boys riding. The kids would be crazy happy. On the corner was a big store, and the owner, Mrs. Womtree was her name, she came over so many times, and when I was short, she brought me food, and sugar, you know, and I never had to pay anything. I was stunned. Some people came in and I knew them, but some people left food at the door or something.

All of them went to the Methodist church or to different churches. We did go to the Methodist church there in Yoncalla, so every time we were in church, and the kids went to the Bible school there, I would stand up and thank everybody. I could not figure out who the food was from, so I would tell them, "Whatever it is, and you brought it, thank you." Later on they put a front new window in the church, and they asked for donations. We were already gone, but I sent money, and they put my name on the little plaque below the window, too.

In the beginning, there was no jobs in Yoncalla, so Lud worked with Melvin, making ditches or putting up stop signs. Later he got a job working on typewriters in Eugene. I didn't work then. The kids were still little, and I stayed with the kids. Lud met somebody in Eugene who worked for the Olympia Company making German and Japanese typewriters, and he said to Lud, "Can you come to California? I have a job for you, and you'll be better paid." So we moved to Los Angeles, California, in 1962. Lud went up and up and up in that company. I worked in California for Bell and Howell in electronics. From California we went to Oklahoma, and Lud was then a service manager and he covered five states, Oklahoma, Kansas, Missouri, Louisiana, and Texas.

The feel was different in Oklahoma. Not for me, but for Lud, because of his skin color. But I could feel that, you know. We were one time in Kansas, Lud had a pass there for school for a machinist, and we went into a restaurant. We sat down there, and we waited and waited and waited and waited, and the waitress went by and by and by with the coffee. She never said, "Hi," "Hello," "You want something?" We were dressed up; we weren't sitting there like, "Give us something for free." I was thinking, "What the hell is your problem?" I could not understand it. I was so stupid then. Well, I was not stupid, stupid, but I thought, "America wouldn't do that." And then Lud told me, "I think they're prejudice over here." He said, "We better walk out. She don't want to serve us." So we drove somewhere else. We got money, and we could eat anywhere. I was always thinking, "When you are that way, I don't need you."

We stayed in Oklahoma for three years, and then from Oklahoma we went back to L.A. The company there merged with another company, so we went back to Oregon, and bought a place there. We stayed in Oregon for another five years. When we came back to Oregon, Litton hired me for electronics, and I built transistors. After that, Lud went over to Continental, and then we went back to L.A., to Hawaii, and then back to Oregon to retire.

I saw a lot of America, and I went back to my country a few times, too. America is so pretty. You have no idea how different it is over here from Belgium. You have to see it to believe it. I came back to Yoncalla a lot of times, and I saw Dr. Emery. Later on she died from bone cancer. The last letter I have from her she said, "See what happened when you put your mind to it?"

Then I called her and I said, "Listen, but it took me a long time."

"Oh," she said, "But that don't make any difference. You made it."

CHAPTER FORTY-TWO

IT'S A BLESSING

MY BROTHER ANTOINE GREW UP HEAVY. HE WAS ALWAYS LIGHT haired with a mustache like a broom. He had lung cancer, and he lost all his teeth. Everybody in Belgium smoked like hell. He drinked, too, and he danced, he went to the cafés on weekends, and he played games. Antoine didn't believe in nothing. He was funny and happy when he got older, but he didn't have a nice childhood. When he came to visit me in America, he talked about growing up.

In Belgium, we always had sabots, Dutch wooden shoes, lying around the house. You walked around your house in slippers, and then you slipped on your wooden shoes to go outside. Antoine said, "When we were young, for punishment Geoff made us sit for hours with our knees in the wooden shoes." In the early times in Belgium, whatever the father tells you, you had to do what he says. Where else were you going to go?

One time Geoff and my mother went out to have a drink. She got drunk and couldn't walk straight or something and she fell. He kicked her and kicked her, "Get up! Get up!"

The boys, Simon and Antoine, grabbed him and said, "Do us a favor. Don't ever touch Mom again. Because that'll be the last time you do."

Antoine told me one time that when he was fifteen Geoff tried to rape him.

I said, "You have to be kidding."

My brother said, "No." He turned around and showed Geoff his fist. "Don't you dare." After that he left, and he never went back again. Antoine was then working and Geoff chased him, the same way he chased me. He said, "I want your money." Antoine said a few things to me, but most of the time he kept quiet about it.

My sister Sarah was to me as stubborn as a mule and short tempered. She had a lousy childhood, that is for sure. She became the cook, she did the wash, and she cleaned the house, whatever I did before I left home. She didn't want to talk about it. Antoine thought she had been molested by Geoff, and so did Lud.

When Sarah was fourteen years old, she was caught with a girlfriend stealing something in a store in Ghent. I was already married when that happened, so she sent me letters to Holland. She told me what happened, that she didn't do it, that the girl put it in her purse, and my sister didn't know. When the police came over to my mother's place, then they saw how the kids were treated. So the government took over and took the kids away from them. I really don't know everything that happened, but Antoine was gone, my sister was sent to a special school, and then I don't know what happened to the other two kids, Simon and Laurent. They never talked about it.

I raised Antoine and Sarah. They knew that something happened, because I never came back when Geoff sent me that letter in Antwerp. They always judged me for that, "Why didn't you come back?" Sarah then started crying.

I said, "This is why I don't talk about it." Geoff was their father, not mine, and I didn't want to hurt her feelings. Sarah was resentful, unhappy, judgmental, all the negative stuff. Everything had to be her way. She didn't believe in God, she didn't believe in anything, and she was always pissed off at everything.

I told her, "Why can't you just be happy?"

"What for?"

I said, "I have no idea. Just because you breathe."

I was like that, too. I hated the whole world. I had stomach pains whenever I was pissed off, and I had to take bicarbonate of soda. You have to get the bitterness out.

A neighbor named Beatrice came and she saw me. Beatrice was in her seventies when I met her, I think. She was real heavy duty, because she got in a car accident somewhere in California, and broke both her legs. She was handicapped, but she could cook and she was clean. I was working then by Litton, and every afternoon around two o'clock I came home, and she sat in her fifth wheel, and she waved to me when I came by, "come over, come over." She always had a Bible with her, and then she would tell me about it.

We talked and talked, and she wanted to know about Lud and me, how we met, and what we did, and why we were in America. She had two daughters, and one died from bone cancer. When her father left and her mother died, there was a doctor there in Indiana, and she worked for the doctor, and in the meantime she got her college education. Beatrice told me her father was an alcoholic, and she talked about it, and that's when I came loose and told her the story about my stepfather.

We met more and more, and then she started working on me. "You shouldn't have the hate like this in your body, because that's not good for you. I have to learn you to get rid of it."

"That would be a miracle," I said. "You know, Beatrice, I don't think I'm going to do it, because I'm a bastard and no good."

And she grabbed my hand and said, "No, you are not a bastard and no good. You are the child of God," she said, "and you are not going to tell me that you hate the whole world either, because you are not the type for that."

I said, "Well, that's what I feel."

Then she told me, "Do me a favor. Whatever it was that hurt you, take the notes, take the pictures, anything that is from that person, burn it and ask the Lord to clean your system out. Forgive him."

I couldn't forgive Geoff, I said. Oh my God, I hated that sucker so bad.

Beatrice said, "That's the pain you have inside. That's the ulcers you have inside. As long as you don't let go of it, then you are an extension of him."

So I did. I took all the letters, I took all of the pictures of Geoff, my mother and my sister, and I burned them in the stove. I said, "Lord, clean my system."

And after that I was so much better. I looked better, I don't have no ulcers, and I was much, much better. The hate was gone, too. I just forgave them. It was not easy. But all those years I cleaned the house, and I did the wash, and I stayed clean on the outside, it was my inside that needed cleaned out.

Mistakes, I did a lot of them, but I learned a lot from them, too. I learned the Lord comes first. Whatever you do, go first to your Father, and I always did. I learned whatever you need, pray for it, and sometimes it will come, and sometimes it doesn't. Now I'm much older, but I see a lot of people from my generation missed the boat, because all that was taught was hate. You'd never guess that Jesus loved you, and it is true. He does. He let you free. But you can not blame Him when you do something wrong.

I went for the first time back to Belgium in 1975, when Lud was sent to Germany by the Olympia Company, about fifteen years since we left for America. I was happy to see the family. But, boy, when I came back, I thought, "Oh, thank God I'm back in America!" My cousin Nathalie and I were always close. She would rather have that I be in Belgium close to her. But I told her, "No, I'm an American citizen, and America is my country. I choose to be here, and I'm never going to go back," you know.

After Antoine, my mother had three other children, but only two of them, Simon, and Laurent survived. The third one, I was his godmother, and I told you about going to his baptism, he died at three months. My aunts and uncles always loved my mother. They stayed away from her because they didn't like Geoff. My mother and Geoff never broke up. Oh, they had disagreements, yes, but broke up, no.

I don't know if Geoff ever changed. My brother said later he did change. They went over to the Jehovah Witnesses, so they went to church in their last days. When Geoff was older, he was purple with arthritis. He couldn't walk no more, he couldn't ride his bicycle no more, so my sister took care of him, and the Jehovah Witnesses took care of him. So I have no idea. If he did change, it's a blessing. If he didn't, I couldn't care less, you know what I mean? Geoff died later, I don't know exactly when. My aunt called and told me.

The first time I went back to Belgium, I went to the house, and then I met my mother for the first time in years. I was there with my cousin Morgane. Geoff opened the door, and my mother was sitting there playing cards. I brought her some stuff. Geoff was standing there and he didn't look at me. He was scared from me, so he always stood away. My mother saw me, she stood up, she hugged me and she cried and cried and cried. She nearly broke me in pieces she hugged me so hard. I told her in her ear, because I don't want nobody to hear, "You know what? I love you, and you know it."

My mother said to me, "I'm happy to see you, because I was always thinking about you."

And I said, "Thank you." I was in shock. She never hugged me like that. So, somewhere, somehow, she was different. A picture of me stood right by her on the window sill. I was looking, and I wanted so badly to take that picture. I should have taken it. My sister later burned it. But at that moment I couldn't. I thought, "No, she is looking at that picture. I'll leave it there." That was the last time that we ever talked to each other.

In the 1980s, she got awful diabetes, and she really had not a nice death, you know. I remember exactly, it was the 16th of February, the day I brought a cake for my two daughters-in-law. I came home from work and I opened my mail box. Then I saw the telegram from Belgium. My mother died. I cried a river. Oh my God, I was in shock.

Funny is that. For all the misery, I loved my mother.